Prabhavathi Meppayil

PACE

5 Reincarnations of the Grid
Michaëla de Lacaze Mohrmann

9 Grids, You Say
Rosalind Krauss

89 Surface Echoes
Mami Kataoka

93 Being with the work and in the work
An Interview with Prabhavathi Meppayil
Wells Fray-Smith

137 List of Works
141 Biography

> Indian artists still go riding on the backs of paradoxes, with the more adventurous of them turning this into an original act of self-definition. Sometimes, with the necessary élan, the ride becomes a critical exercise prodding the modern itself or, rather, the fixed notions of that category, to diversify its possibilities outside the Western mainstream. Geeta Kapur[1]

Paradox, as suggested by the influential voice of art historian Geeta Kapur, is often a hallmark of great contemporary Indian art that reconsiders modernism—its forms as well as its polemics—through India's fraught postcolonial experience of modernization. Proving this rule, the art of Prabhavathi Meppayil takes critical paradoxicality to new and exceptional heights, as the following pages explore. More comprehensive than past publications on Meppayil, this book places the artist's most recent pieces alongside works stretching back to 2010 to capture her oeuvre's sustained interweaving of the modernist canon with histories and practices that fall outside of it. A conversation between curator Wells Fray-Smith and Meppayil sheds additional light on the latter's artistic evolution and creative process by tracking the many ways her art "destabilizes fixed categories," as Fray-Smith observes. Counterbalancing scholars' tendency to acknowledge the artist's excavation of Indian culture without ever following her into these depths, an essay by curator Mami Kataoka examines Meppayil's reductivist abstraction through the cosmologies of Buddhism and Jainism. Finally, readers will find a re-publication of Rosalind Krauss's consequential essay "Grids, You Say," originally written for Pace Gallery's 1978 exhibition catalogue *Grids: Format and Image in 20th Century Art.*

Considering art historians, most notably Benjamin H. D. Buchloh, have meticulously analyzed Meppayil's antinomic redeployment of the grid, as well as other germane modernist paradigms such as the monochrome, Krauss's reprint might be viewed as needlessly yoking Meppayil's work to accounts of European and North American art.[2] Far from being such a heavy-handed and hegemonizing maneuver, the foregrounding of Krauss's text is meant as an invitation to further parse Meppayil's paradoxical production in light of her geographic and cultural specificity, because the grid's inherent contradictions—or "schizophrenia," as Krauss puts it—offer a site of intervention for artists like Meppayil. It is in the grid's and, by extension, modernism's incongruities that artists from the Global South can often loosen the threads of an overly neat (and exclusionary) modernist narrative, thereby creating spaces for their histories and, above all, futures. In fact, these other(ed) stories and regions are at times already repressed within some of these seminal art-historical texts such as "Grids, You Say," for instance.

In her essay, Krauss tallies all the ways in which the lattice is at odds with itself: it is materialist yet transcendental, secular but sacred, temporal as well as spatial, and simultaneously centrifugal and centripetal. Its novelty to twentieth-century artists sprung from the fact that it "appear[s] nowhere, nowhere at all, in the art of the last [century]," Krauss argues. It exists only covertly in nineteenth-century Symbolist paintings of barred windows—reflective and opaque entities sufficiently multivalent to count as ancestors of the modernist grid. However, this origin is more complex than what Krauss acknowledges. Throughout the nineteenth century, the industrial revolution had gradually improved the production of glass from diminutive pieces to expansive sheets. This technological feat led to the Great Exhibition's famous crystal architecture in 1851 and, more mundanely, to homes with single-pane windows, unobstructed by a grid of muntins. With this in mind, Symbolism's paintings of barred windows become melancholic portrayals of a vanishing, pre-industrial craft and architectural style. They also capture another trend: the persistent desire for multipaned windows, which until today used muntins not out of structural necessity but owing to a nostalgic appetite for decoration and craftmanship. It is here, then, in Krauss's chosen Symbolist genesis of the modernist grid that we can locate an additional core contradiction of the grid, one that Krauss never mentions: the grid, despite its undeniable austerity as a basic matrix connotative of science and technological progress, is also an instance of pre-industrial, artisanal ornamentation.

Once viewed through the prism of handmade embellishment, the grid actually appears everywhere in time and space: French cathedral floors, ancient Greek coffered ceilings, Arabic screens, Portuguese *azulejos*, and Aztec codices. India, too, as Meppayil is likely to know, has its fair share of ornate grids, as evidenced by Jain manuscripts of Rajasthan and Gujarat origin, and sacred *kōlams* that build floral patterns through a precise grid of dots symbolizing the origin of cosmic order. Even in the Rig Veda and the Upanishads the universe is conceived as a continuous fabric, whose warp and weft constitute a splendorous grid pattern woven by the gods themselves.

The grid's split identity as spartan yet decorative, and of the machine-made present but also of the handwrought past, could not, of course, be more troublesome to the North Atlantic's modernist art and architecture, which rely so heavily on the grid while recurrently denigrating the ornamental as criminal and obsolescent, as the decadent and frivolous visual language of women and non-Western cultures alike.[3] Yet many works by white twentieth-century artists who built their oeuvres on the grid obliquely gesture to these prior, more decorative non-European apparitions of the grid. For all its strict orthogonal regularity, *Friendship* (1963) by Agnes Martin—whose spare grids are often compared to Meppayil's—makes such a sumptuous use of hand-applied gold leaf that its incised rows of rectangles evoke, for example, the Byzantine golden mosaics adorning the Hagia Sophia's doorways. Gego, whom Buchloh mentions in relation to Meppayil, also created her *Tejeduras* by interlacing golden cigarette wrappers into gridded patterns that nod to the embellished latticework of baskets woven by present-day Amazonian tribes.[4] Other examples abound, from the glass grids of Josef Albers and textile ones of Anni Albers to the groundbreaking painted grids of Joaquín Torres-García, who, like the Alberses, found inspiration in Pre-Columbian textiles and architecture.

None, however, is more clear-eyed about this particular duality of the grid than Meppayil, whose work stages the grid's twin asceticism and decorativeness with the dramatic force of a phenomenological encounter. From a distance, her gridded, monochromatic paintings and installations evince a soberness and orthogonal exactitude epitomizing a modernist aesthetic. The viewer thus remains unprepared for the finery harbored by her works. Myriad details—the asymmetrical shapes and floral patterns of found tools; the shimmer of gold and chromatic bleed of oxidizing copper wires; richly haptic imprints of *thinnams*—are only discovered up close, as if to better overwhelm the eye and tempt the fingers. These elements cannot be mistaken as anything else but ornamental in nature, especially since Meppayil links them to Bangalore's jewelry district and to her own family's multigenerational goldsmithing business, thereby recoding the decorative in positive terms.[5] "When the molds are reiterated as art objects," she notes, "it is difficult to solely read them as Minimalist, simple forms because they come with individual histories that I want to engage with."[6]

Through its gradual, theatrical revelation of ornamentality, Meppayil's work stages a return of the repressed not only in terms of the modernist grid but also with regard to Minimalism. Though Meppayil is frequently linked to this movement, its practitioners abhorred any belaboring of surfaces, any trace of the hand—a fact not lost on Meppayil. With her concrete, cubic sculptures bearing incised, copper-lined shapes similar to her

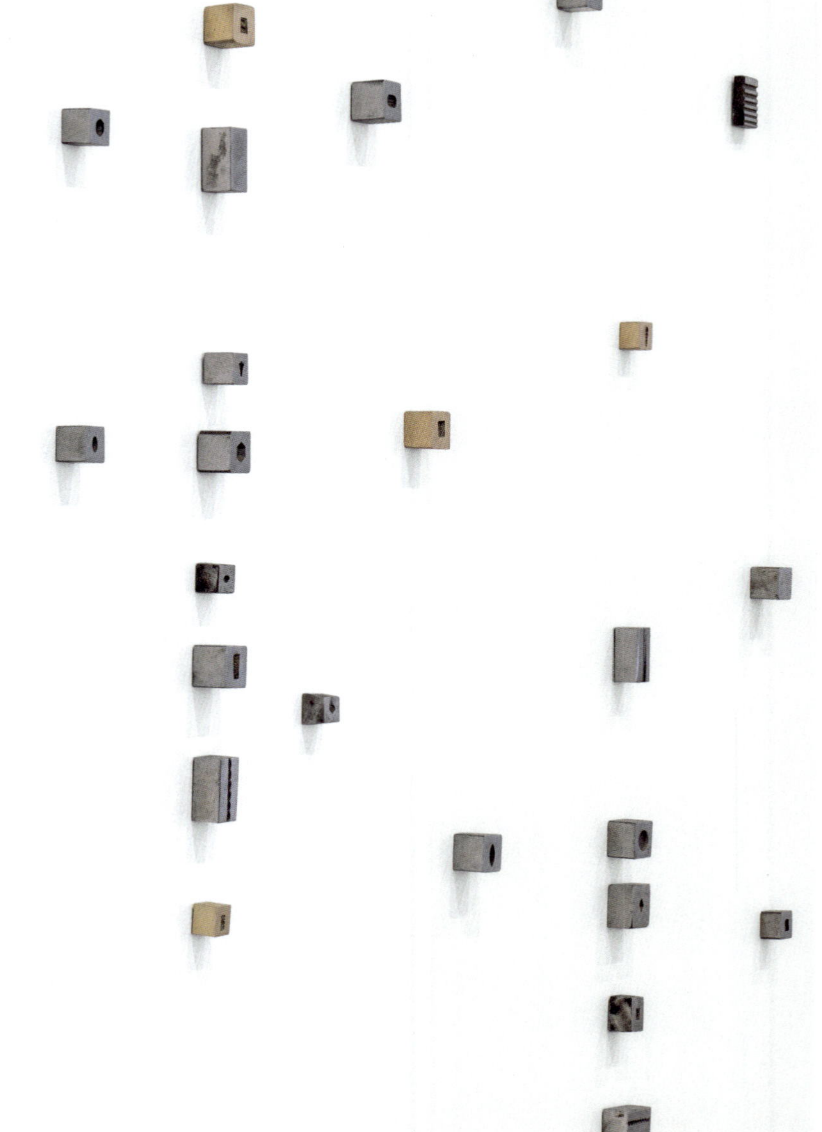

sb/eighteen, 2018 (detail)

father's goldsmithing molds in *sb/eighteen* (2018) (pp. 42–43), Meppayil riffs on Donald Judd's specific object, turning the Minimalist cube—that industrially made thing symbolic of U.S.-corporate capitalism and its neocolonial aspirations[7]—into its opposite: a monumentalized artisanal tool, an homage to India's age-old tradition of goldsmithing and jewelry-making.[8] Is this a mournful, mnemonic gesture or an act of celebratory affirmation, even resistance?

To Buchloh, Meppayil's art orchestrates an ambiguous confrontation between "elements of a highly differentiated manual dexterity of the past," and "omens of the imminent technical control and exclusion of tactile, artisanal, and musical forms."[9] Yet he hardly conceals his pessimism regarding the outcome of this confrontation, no matter how ambiguous. The artisanal components of Meppayil's art are, in his words, "residue[s] of a disappearing, if not already lost, external world that can only be rescued in the form of the accidental fragment." In Buchloh's analysis the "manifest obsolescence" of the modernist forms that Meppayil resurrects is mirrored by her "almost melancholic" artisanal tools, which seem similarly doomed.[10]

But is the dismal fate of once utopian modernist strategies truly the ineluctable future of India's visual cultures and crafts and its traditional ways of life? In her interview with Fray-Smith, Meppayil delights in pointing out the energetic sounds of goldsmiths working in her studio's neighborhood—sounds indexed by her paintings' rhythmic markings and so lively as to be audible on an international phone call with Fray-Smith. Consider also the continuity of still widely worn Indian "temple jewelry" or how the goldsmith in India is a hallowed professional, responsible for crafting *and* blessing the *thaali*: the apotropaic gold chain presented at weddings to ensure—of all things—longevity. This broader context of goldsmithing so skillfully belied by the conceptual tenor and Minimalist style of Meppayil's work is nonetheless evoked by its materials, tools, and the sounds guiding its production. The artist seeks to maintain this ambiguity and this fraught paradox. She explains:

> My work is often read as being about the artist, the practice, and the craft because I come from a family of goldsmiths and because that history is there, but it's not as simple as that. *I am critically engaging with the language of the work through the context of my lived experience. This is where the histories of artisanal practice, or personal narratives, come into the picture and overlap with the visible geometric vocabulary.*[11]

In other words, Meppayil is not out to merely revive Indian artisanship. Rather, she is pursuing the interweaving of past and present, of artisanal practice and geometric Minimalist vocabularies. Her work—and this is where its conceptual dexterity becomes apparent—seeks to transcend the simplistic opposition between outmodedness and contemporaneity.

Buchloh's view of late capitalism's "regimes of total determination and control" is, ironically, so fatalistic that it performs the very domination it rails against. Meppayil's copper wires come to evoke an "invasive ... expanding electronic and technical order," which domineers everyday existence.[12] Yet India is also negotiating this technological order on its own terms by becoming a hotbed for homegrown tech startups, as Kataoka notes in her essay.[13] Too taken by his visions of totalizing forces, Buchloh fails to see the futurity encapsulated in India's time-honored crafts. True, Meppayil's art points to "conditions of rapidly advancing reification," that is, to global capital's threat to ways of life metonymically suggested by the artisanship present in her work.[14] Nonetheless, her art simultaneously alludes to the awesome endurance of Indian craft-based traditions—traditions that have been reinvigorated, not decimated, by foreign incursions for a staggering 5,000 years. This is the paradoxical intervention of Meppayil's oeuvre: that the tired modernist grid may finally be reaching a bright future by riding on the back of India's ancient decorative crafts, and vice versa.

1 Geeta Kapur, *When Was Modernism: Essays on Contemporary Cultural Practice in India* (New Delhi: Tulika, 2007), 147.
2 See Benjamin H. D. Buchloh, "Prabhavathi Meppayil: Redeeming Abstraction (under Duress)," *Prabhavathi Meppayil: nine seventeen* (New York: Pace Gallery, 2014).
3 See, for instance, Adolf Loos's 1908 essay "Ornament and Crime."
4 Buchloh, 47.
5 Meppayil's reframing of the ornamental also amounts to a revalorization of its many cognates, for example, the "feminine," the "primitive," and the "oriental," which are terms used to unfairly disparage cultures and practices falling outside of Europe and North America's patriarchal societies. It should also not be lost on readers that Meppayil's very use of thinnams and goldsmithing techniques counts as a subtle feminist gesture given that India's goldsmithing trade is dominated by men and passed on from father to son—a fact surely not lost on Meppayil, the daughter of a goldsmith.
6 Prabhavathi Meppayil quoted in Wells Fray-Smith, "Being with the work and in the work," this volume, 95.
7 See Anna C. Chave, "Minimalism and the Rhetoric of Power," *Arts Magazine* 64.5 (January 1990), 44–63.
8 Meppayil attests, "When the molds are reiterated as art objects, it is difficult to solely read them as Minimalist, simple forms because they come with individual histories that I want to engage with. Unlike the industrial objects of the 1970s, these molds are handmade and used by individuals; there is a human touch. The socio-cultural history and context of the objects add layers to the complexity of the language." Fray-Smith, 95.
9 Buchloh, 48.
10 Ibid., 48, 51, 44.
11 Fray-Smith, 95. My emphasis.
12 Buchloh, 41, 46.
13 See Mami Kataoka, "Surface Echoes," this volume, 90.
14 Buchloh, 44.

Grids, You Say Rosalind Krauss

Grids?—you say—What is there to write or to read about grids? Hasn't everything been said already? Isn't it true that nowadays one must, in order to add anything at all, move into those equally arid spaces: the very academic or the very technical?—By which you point to the way that grids do not appear to be the suitable subject for discussion, seeming to be beyond—or is it above, or below?—discourse. Grids, we think, are inimical to the space of the page on which writing or reading takes place, because that page is one we can imaginatively inhabit. In their position as emblems of all that is quintessentially modern in art, grids are like that other symptom of modernity, the large city. As with the teeming metropolis, the grid is fine to visit—to look at (quickly)—but one wouldn't want to live there—in the sense that habitation, like reading, takes time.

Yet whether this gives us pleasure or pain, grids *are* the emblems of modernity, and so we must find a way of discussing them, of making their space and that of the page more available to one another. Here is one attempt.

When I was a teenager I saw a play called *Inherit the Wind*, a play that was intended, in theatrical parlance, as an actor's vehicle, for it staged the gladiatorial combat between two great figures, William Jennings Bryan and Clarence Darrow, as they clashed in a spectacle of oratory in the arena of the Scopes trial. From my place, sitting in the audience, I found the actors, going through their paces of declamatory vehemence or implacable determination, admirable; but I found the ostensible matter of the play completely bizarre. For between Darwin's theory of evolution and the biblical scene of Creation, as an explanation of how man arrived on this planet, there did not seem to be a serious choice. It was obvious to me that whatever role the story of Genesis had to play, in my or anyone else's spiritual life, it had to be highly symbolical. And from my adolescent perspective, this forced march of the spiritual into the realm of the purely fictitious did not strike me as much of a problem. So when the William Jennings Bryan character, exercised over the man-from-monkey issue to the point of heart attack, thundered from his stretcher that we would "inherit the wind," I found it rather comic. There is, of course, a way to find it *seriously* comic—although I was too young to know that at the time. Nietzsche spoke of it this way when he wrote, "We wished to awaken the feeling of man's sovereignty by showing his divine birth: this path is now forbidden, since a monkey stands at the entrance."

But if the split between spirit and matter that was presided over by nineteenth-century science is what became the legitimate heritage of twentieth-century schoolchildren, it is no less the heritage of twentieth-century art. And the grid is its emblematic form.

There are two ways in which the grid functions to declare the modernity of modern art. One is spatial; the other is temporal. In the spatial sense, the grid states the absolute autonomy of the realm of art. Flattened, geometricized, ordered, it is anti-natural, anti-mimetic, anti-real. It is what art looks like when it turns its back on nature. In the flatness that results from its coordinates, the grid is the means of crowding out the dimensions of the real and replacing them with the lateral spread of a single surface. In the over-all regularity of its organization, it is the result not of imitation, but of aesthetic decree. Insofar as its order is that of pure relationship, the grid is a way of abrogating the claims of natural objects to have an order particular to themselves; the relationships in the aesthetic field are shown by the grid to be *sui generis* and, with respect to natural objects, to be both prior and final. The grid declares the space of art to be at once autonomous and autotelic.

In the temporal dimension, the grid is an emblem of modernity by being just that: the form that is ubiquitous in the art of *our* century, while appearing nowhere, nowhere at all, in the art of the last one. In that great set of chain reactions by which modernism was born out of the efforts of the nineteenth century, one final shift resulted in breaking the chain. By "discovering" the grid, Cubism, De Stijl, Mondrian, Malevich ... landed in a place that was out of reach of everything that went before. Which is to say, they landed in the present, and everything else was declared to be the past.

One has to travel a long way back into the history of art to find previous examples of grids. One has to go to the fifteenth and sixteenth centuries, to treatises on perspective and to those exquisite studies by Uccello or Leonardo or Dürer, where the perspective lattice is inscribed on the depicted world as the armature of its organization. But perspective studies are not really early instances of grids. Perspective was, after all, the science of the real, not the mode of withdrawal from it. Perspective was the demonstration of the way reality and its representation could be mapped onto one another, the way the painted image and its real-world referent did in fact relate to one another—the first being a form of knowledge about the second. Everything about the grid opposes that relationship, cuts it off from the very beginning. Unlike perspective, the grid does not map the space of a room or a landscape or a group of figures onto the surface of a painting. Indeed, if it maps anything, it maps the surface of the painting itself. It is a transfer in which nothing changes place. The material qualities of the surface, we could say, are mapped onto the aesthetic dimensions of the same surface. And those two planes—the material and the aesthetic—are demonstrated to be the same plane: coextensive, and, through the abscissas and ordinates of the grid, coordinate. Considered in this way, the bottom line of the grid is a naked and determined materialism.

But if it is materialism that the grid would make us talk about—and there seems no other logical way to discuss it—that is not the way that artists have ever discussed it. Open any tract—*Plastic Art and Pure Plastic Art* or *The Non-Objective World*, for instance—and you will find that Mondrian and Malevich are not discussing canvas or pigment or graphite or any other form of matter. They are talking about Being or Mind or Spirit. From their point of view, the grid is a staircase to the Universal, and they are not interested in what happens below in the Concrete. Or, to take a more up-to-date example, we could think about Ad Reinhardt who, despite his repeated insistence that "Art is art," ended up by painting a series of black nine-square grids in which the motif that inescapably emerges is a Greek cross. And there is no painter in the West who can be unaware of the symbolic power of the cruciform shape and the Pandora's box of spiritual reference that is opened once you use it.

And this brings us back to Scopes and the monkey trial and William Jennings Bryan. For if that trial is a symbol of the absolute rift in the modern world between the sacred and the secular, then we might want to ask: on which side of that split did art come down? And the answer is: it's hard to say. Hard, not because we can't tell the one from the other, but because, art seems to have decided for both. In the increasingly de-sacralized space of the nineteenth century, art became the refuge for religious emotion; it became, as it has remained, a secular form of religion. Although this condition could be discussed openly in the late nineteenth century, it is something that is inadmissible in the twentieth, so that by now we find it indescribably embarrassing to mention "art" and "spirit" in the same sentence.

And the peculiar power of the grid, its extraordinary long life in the specialized space of modern art, arises from its potential to preside over this shame: to mask and to reveal it at one and the same time. In the cultist space of modern art, the grid serves not only as emblem but also as myth. For like all myths, it deals with paradox or contradiction not by dissolving the paradox or resolving the contradiction, but by covering them over so that they seem (but only seem)

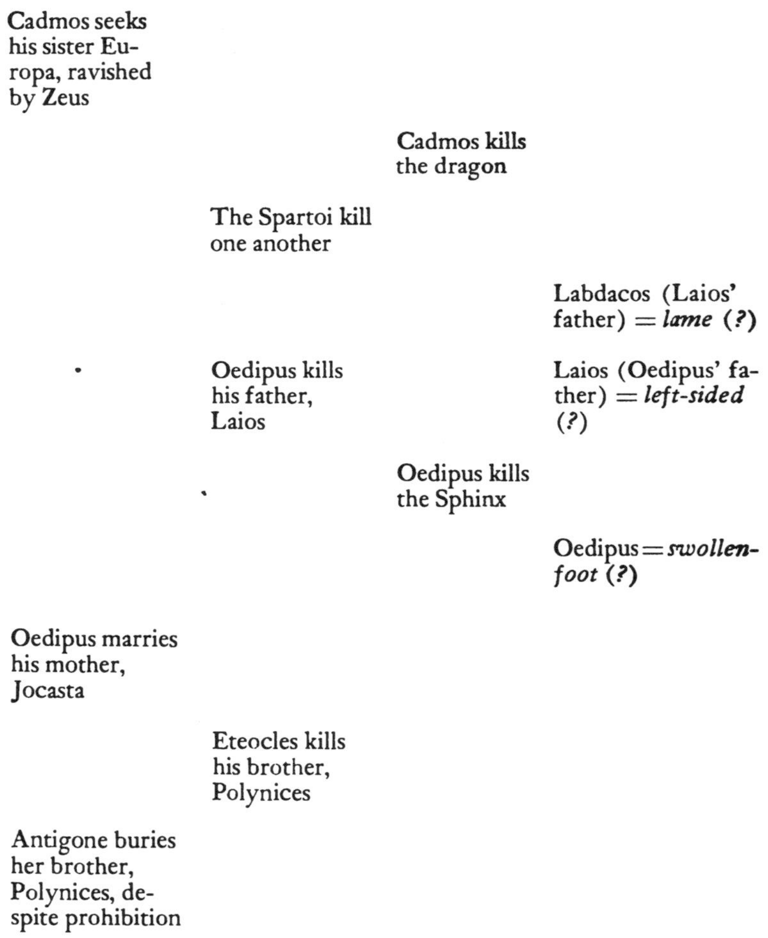

Cadmos seeks his sister Europa, ravished by Zeus			
		Cadmos kills the dragon	
	The Spartoi kill one another		
			Labdacos (Laios' father) = *lame* (?)
	Oedipus kills his father, Laios		**Laios (Oedipus' father) = *left-sided* (?)**
		Oedipus kills the Sphinx	
			Oedipus = *swollen-foot* (?)
Oedipus marries his mother, Jocasta			
	Eteocles kills his brother, Polynices		
Antigone buries her brother, Polynices, despite prohibition			

Claude Lévi-Strauss, structural diagram of the Oedipus mythemes from *Structural Anthropology* (copyright © 1963. Reprinted by permission of Basic Books, an imprint of Hachette Book Group, Inc.)

to go away. The grid's mythic power is that it makes us able to think we are dealing with materialism (or sometimes science, or logic) while at the same time it provides us with a release into belief (or illusion, or fiction). The work of Reinhardt or Agnes Martin would be instances of this power. And one of the important sources of this power is the way the grid is, as I have said before, so stridently modern to look at, seeming to have left no place of refuge, no room on the face of it, for vestiges of the nineteenth century to hide.

In suggesting that the success[1] of the grid is somehow connected to its structure as myth, I may of course be accused of stretching a point beyond the limits of common sense, since myths are stories, and like all narratives they unravel through time, whereas grids are not only spatial to start with, they are visual structures that explicitly reject a narrative or sequential reading of any kind. But the notion of myth I am using here depends on a structuralist mode of analysis, by which the sequential features of a story are rearranged to form a spatial organization.[2]

The reason the structuralists do this is that they wish to understand the function of myths; and this function they see as the cultural attempt to deal with contradiction. By spatializing the story, into vertical columns for example, they are able to display the features of the contradiction and to show how these underlie the attempts of a specific mythical tale to paper-over this opposition with narrative. Thus, in analyzing a variety of creation myths, Lévi-Strauss finds the presence of a conflict between earlier notions of man's origins as a process of autochthony (man born from the earth, like plants), and later ones involving the sexual relations between two parents. Because the earlier forms of belief are sacrosanct they must be maintained even though they violate common sense views about sexuality and birth. The function of the myth is to allow *both* views to be held in some kind of para-logical suspension.

The justification of this violation of the temporal dimension of the myth arises, then, from the results of structural analysis: namely, the sequential progress of the story does not achieve resolution but rather, repression. That is, for a given culture, the contradiction is a powerful one, one that will not go away, but will only go, so to speak, underground. So the vertical columns of structuralist analysis are a way of unearthing the unmanageable oppositions that promoted the making of the myth in the first place. We could analogize this procedure to that of psychoanalysis, where the "story" of a life is similarly seen as an attempt to resolve primal contradictions that nevertheless remain in the structure of the unconscious. Because they are there as repressed elements, they function to promote endless repetitions of the same conflict. Thus another rationale for the vertical columns (the spatialization of the "story") emerges from the fact that it is useful to see the way each feature of the story (for structuralist analysis these are called mythemes) burrows down, independently, into the historical past: in the case of psychoanalysis this is the past of the individual; for the analysis of myth, this is the past of the culture or the tribe.

Therefore, although the grid is certainly not a story, it *is* a structure, and one, moreover, that allows a contradiction between the values of science and those of belief to maintain themselves within the consciousness of modernism, or rather its unconscious, as something repressed. In order to continue its analysis—to assess the very success of the grid's capacities to repress—we might follow the lead of the two analytical procedures I have just mentioned. This would mean burrowing along the site of each part of the contradiction down into its historical foundations. No matter how absent the grid was in nineteenth-century art, it is precisely into these historical grounds that we must go to find its sources.

Now, although the grid itself is invisible in nineteenth-century painting, it was not entirely absent from a certain kind of accessory literature to which that painting paid an increasing amount of attention. This is the literature of physiological optics. By the nineteenth century the study of optics had split into two parts. One half consisted of the analysis of light and its physical properties: its motion; its refractive features as it was passed through lenses, for example: its capacity to be quantified, or measured. In conducting such studies, scientists presupposed that these were features of light as such, that is, light as it existed independent of human (or animal) perception.

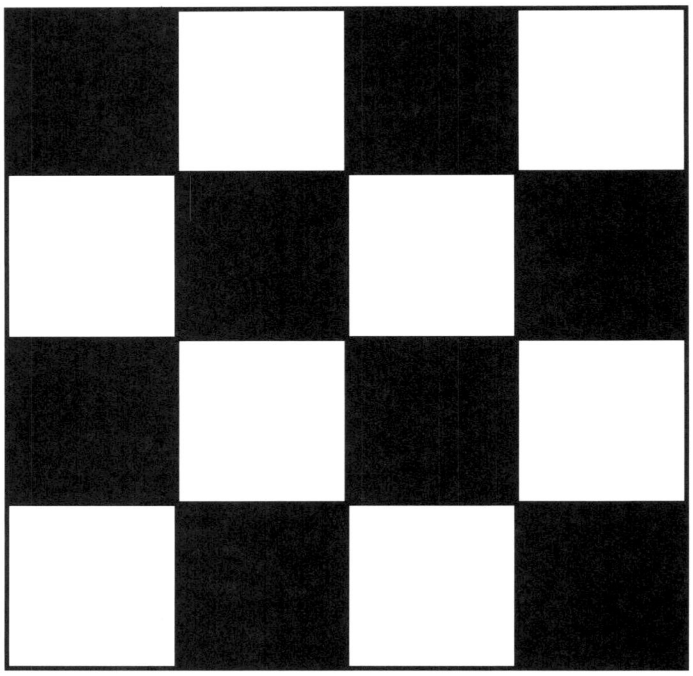

The second branch of optics concentrated on the physiology of the perceiving mechanism; it was concerned with light and color as they are seen. And it is this branch of optics that was of immediate concern to artists.

Whatever their sources of information—whether Chevreul, or Charles Blanc, or Rood or Helmholtz, or even Goethe[3]—painters had to confront a particular fact: the physiological screen through which light passes to the human brain is not transparent, like a window pane; it is, like a filter, involved in a set of specific distortions. For us, as human perceivers, there is an unbreachable gulf between "real" color and "seen" color. We may be able to measure the first; but we can only experience the second. And this is because, among other things, color is always involved in interaction—one color reading onto and affecting its neighbor. Even if we are only looking at a single color, there is still interaction, because the retinal excitation of the after-image will superimpose on the first chromatic stimulus that of a second, which is its complementary. The whole issue of complementary colors, along with the whole edifice of color harmonics that painters constructed on its basis, was thus a matter of physiological optics.

Johann Wolfgang von Goethe, *Theory of Colors*, trans. Charles Eastlake (London, 1840)

The interesting feature of treatises written on physiological optics is that they were illustrated with grids. Because it was a matter of demonstrating the interaction of specific particles throughout a continuous field, that field was analyzed into the modular and repetitive structure of the grid. So for the artist who wished to enlarge his understanding of vision in the direction of science, the grid was there as a matrix of knowledge. By its very abstraction, the grid conveyed one of the basic laws of this knowledge—the separation of the perceptual screen from that of the "real" world. Given all of this, it is not surprising that the grid—as an emblem of the infrastructure of vision—should become an increasingly insistent and visible feature of Neo-Impressionist painting, as Seurat, Signac, Cross and Luce applied themselves to the lessons of physiological optics. Just as it is not surprising that the more they applied these lessons, the more "abstract" their art became, so that as the critic Félix Fénéon observed of the work of Seurat, science began to yield its opposite, which is Symbolism.

Now Symbolism itself stood adamantly opposed to any traffic at all between art and science, or for that matter, between art and "reality." Symbolism's object was metaphysical understanding, not the mundane; and it was interested in those aspects of culture that were interpretations rather than imitations of the real. And so Symbolist art would be the last place, we might think, to look for even an incipient version of grids. But once again we would be wrong.

The grid appears in Symbolist art in the form of windows, the material presence of their panes expressed by the geometrical intervention of the window's mullions. The Symbolist interest in windows clearly reaches back into the early nineteenth century, and Romanticism.[4] But in the hands of the Symbolist painters and poets, this image is turned in an explicitly modernist direction. For the window is experienced as simultaneously transparent and opaque.

As a transparent vehicle, the window is that which admits light—or Spirit—into the initial darkness of the room. Yet if glass transmits, it also reflects. And so the window is experienced by the Symbolist as a mirror as well—something that freezes and locks the self into the space of its own reduplicated being. Flowing and freezing; *glace* in French means glass, mirror and ice: transparency, opacity, and water. In the associative system of Symbolist thought this liquidity points in two directions. First, towards the flow of birth—

the amniotic fluid, the "source"—but then, towards the freezing into stasis or death—the sterile immobility of the mirror. For Mallarmé, particularly, the window functioned as this complex, polysemic sign by which he could also project the "crystallization of reality into art."[5] Mallarmé's *Les Fenêtres* dates from 1863; Redon's most evocative window, *Le Jour*, appeared in 1891 in the volume *Songes*.

If the window is this matrix of ambi- or multi-valence, and the bars of the windows—the grid—are what help us to see, to focus on, this matrix, they are themselves the symbol of the Symbolist work of art. They function as the multi-level representative through which the work of art can allude, and even reconstitute, the forms of Being.

I do not think it is an exaggeration to say that behind every twentieth-century grid, there lies—like a trauma that must be repressed—a Symbolist window parading in the guise of a treatise on optics. Once we realize this, we can also understand that in twentieth-century art there are "grids" even where we do not expect to find them—in the art of Matisse, for example (his *Windows*), which only admits openly to the grid in the final stages of the *papiers découpés*.

Because of its bivalent structure (and history) the grid is fully, even cheerfully, schizophrenic. I have witnessed and participated in arguments about whether the grid portends the centrifugal or centripetal existence of the work of art.[6] Logically speaking, the grid extends, in all directions, to infinity. Any boundaries imposed upon it by a given painting or sculpture, can only be seen—according to this logic—as arbitrary. By virtue of the grid, the given work of art is presented as a mere fragment, a tiny piece arbitrarily cropped from an infinitely larger fabric. Thus the grid operates from the work of art outward, compelling our acknowledgement of a world beyond the frame. This is the centrifugal reading. The centripetal one works, naturally enough, from the outer limits of the aesthetic object inward. The grid is, in relation to *this* reading, a re-presentation of everything that separates the work of art from the world, from ambient space and from other objects. The grid is an introjection of the boundaries of the work onto the interior of the image; it is a mapping of the space inside the frame onto itself. It is a mode of repetition, the content of which is the conventional nature of art itself.

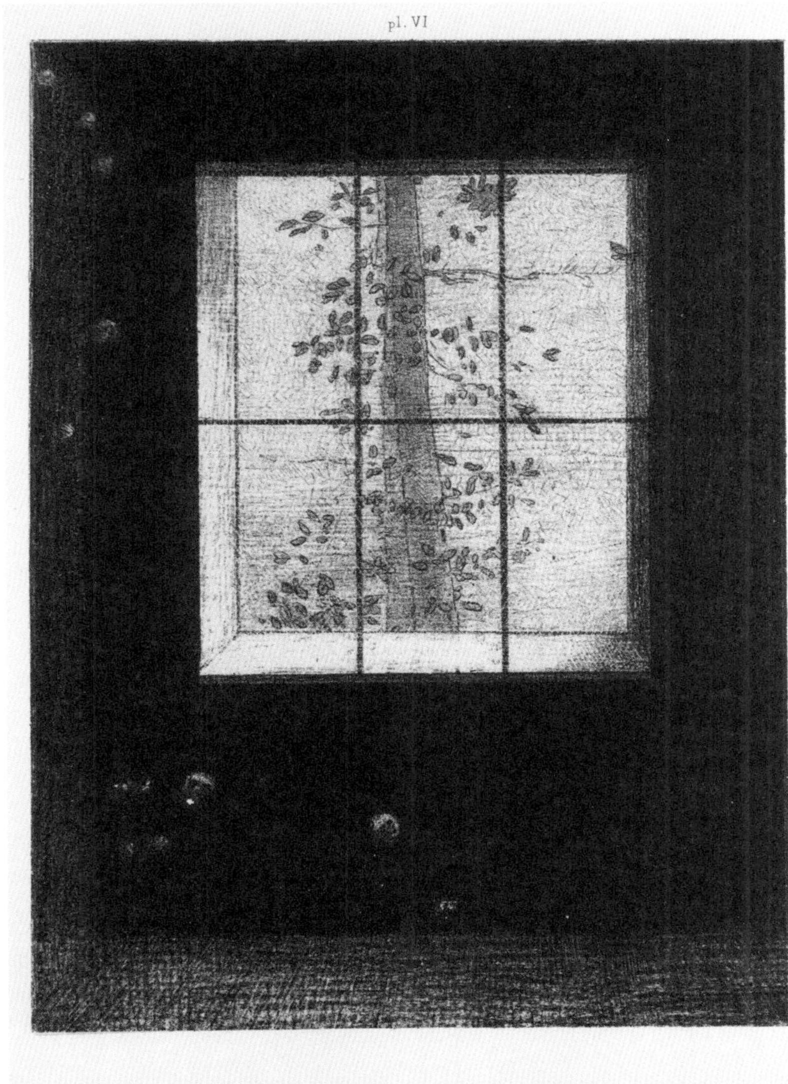

Odilon Redon, *Day (Le Jour)*, from the series, *Dreams (Songes)*, plate VI, 1891. Lithograph on chine collé; only state. Image: 8 ¼ × 6 ⅛" (21 × 15.6 cm), sheet: 17 ⅝ × 12 7/16" (44.8 × 31.6 cm) The Metropolitan Museum of Art, New York. Rogers Fund, 1920

The work of Mondrian, taken together with its various and conflicting readings, is a perfect example of this dispute. Is what we see in a particular painting merely a section of an implied continuity, or is the painting structured as an autonomous, organic whole? Given the visual, or formal, consistency of Mondrian's mature style and the passion of his theoretical pronouncements, we would think that work of this sort would have to hold to one position or the other—and because the chosen position contains a definition about the very nature and goals of art, one would think that an artist would certainly not want to confuse the issue by seeming to imply both. Yet that is exactly what Mondrian does.

There are certain paintings that are overwhelmingly centrifugal, particularly the vertical and horizontal grids seen within diamond-shaped canvases—the contrast between frame and grid enforcing the sense of fragmentation, as though we were looking at a landscape through a window, the frame of the window arbitrarily truncating our view but never shaking our certainty that the landscape continues beyond the limits of what we can, at that moment, see. But other works, even from the same years, are just as explicitly centripetal. In these, the black lines forming the grid are never allowed actually to reach the outer margins of the work, and this cesura between the outer limits of the grid and the outer limits of the painting forces us to read the one as completely contained within the other.

Because the centrifugal argument posits the theoretical continuity of the work of art with the world, it can support many different ways of using the grid—ranging from purely abstract statements of this continuity to projects which order aspects of "reality"—that reality itself conceived more or less abstractly. Thus at the more abstract end of this spectrum we find explorations of the perceptual field (an aspect of Agnes Martin's or Larry Poons's use of the grid), or of phonic interactions (the grids of Patrick Ireland), and as we move towards the less abstract we find statements about the infinite expansion of man-made sign systems (the numbers and alphabets of Jasper Johns). Moving further in the direction of the concrete, we find work that organizes "reality" by means of photographic integers (Warhol and, in a different manner, Chuck Close) as well as work that is, in part, a meditation on architectural space (Louise Nevelson or Lucas Samaras, for example). At this point the three-dimensional grid (now, a lattice) is understood as a theoretical model of architectural space in general, some small piece of which can be given material form, and at the opposite poles of this kind of thinking we find the decorative projects of Frank Lloyd Wright and the work of De Stijl practitioners like Rietveld or Vantongerloo. (Sol LeWitt's modules and lattices are a later manifestation of this position.)

And of course, for the centripetal practice, the opposite is true. Concentrating on the surface of the work as something complete and internally organized, the centripetal branch of practice tends not to dematerialize that surface, but to make it itself the object of vision. And here again one finds one of those curious paradoxes by which the use of the grid is marked at every turn. The beyond-the-frame attitude, in addressing the world and its structure, would seem to trace its lineage back to the nineteenth century in relation to the operations of science, and thus to carry the positivist or materialist implications of its heritage. The within-the-frame attitude, on the contrary, involved as it is with the purely conventional and autotelic reading of the work of art, would seem to issue from purely Symbolist origins, and thus to carry all those readings which we oppose to "science" or "materialism"—readings which inflect the work as symbolic, cosmological, spiritual, vitalist. Yet we know that by and large this is not true. Through a kind of short-circuiting of this logic, the within-the-frame grids are generally far more materialist in character (take such different examples as Alfred Jensen and Frank Stella); while the beyond-the-frame examples often entail the dematerialization of the surface, the dispersal of matter into perceptual flicker or implied motion. And we also know that this schizophrenia allows for many artists—from Mondrian, to Albers, to Kelly, to LeWitt, to think about the grid in both ways at once.

In discussing the operation and character of the grid within the general field of modern art I have had recourse to words like "repression" and "schizophrenia." Since these terms are being applied to a cultural phenomenon and not to individuals, they are obviously not intended in their literal, clinical sense, but only analogically: to compare the structure of one thing to the structure of another. The terms of this analogy were clear, I hope, from the discussion of the parallel structures and functions of both grids and myths.

But one further aspect of this analogy still needs to be brought out; and that is the way in which this psychological terminology functions at some distance from that of *history*. What I mean is that we speak of the aetiology of a psychological condition, not the history of it. History, as we normally use it, implies the connection of events through time, a sense of inevitable change as we move from one event to the next, and the cumulative effect of change which is itself qualitative, so that we tend to view history as *developmental*. Aetiology is not developmental. It is rather an investigation into the conditions necessary for one specific change—the acquisition of disease—to take place. In that sense aetiology is more like looking into the background of a chemical experiment, by asking when and how a given group of elements came together to effect a new compound or to precipitate

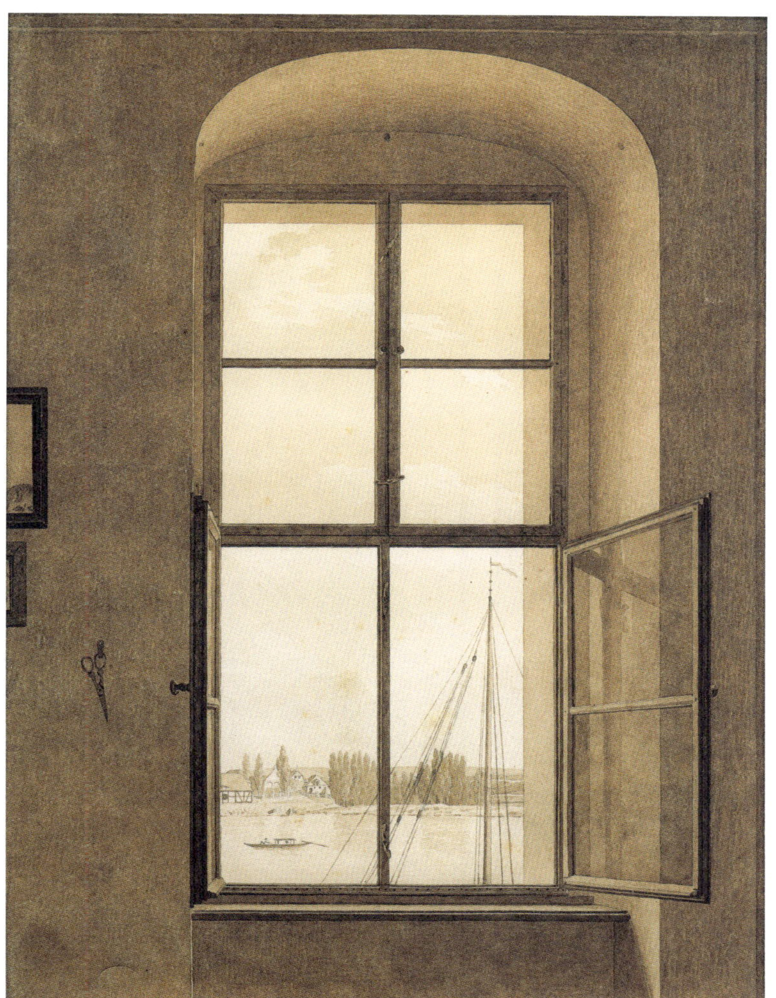

Caspar David Friedrich, *View from the artist's studio (right window)*, 1805–06. Sepia on paper, 12¼ × 9⁵⁄₁₆" (31.2 × 23.7 cm). Österreichische Galerie Belvedere, Vienna

something out of a liquid. With the aetiology of neuroses, we may take a "history" of the individual, to explore what went into the formation of the neurotic structure; but once the neurosis is formed, we are specifically enjoined from thinking in terms of "development," and instead we speak of repetition.

With regard to the advent of the grid in twentieth-century art, there is, it seems to me, the need to think aetiologically rather than historically. Certain conditions combined to precipitate the grid into a position of aesthetic pre-eminence. We can speak of what those things are and how they came together throughout the nineteenth century, and then spot the moment of chemical combination, so to speak, in the early decades of the twentieth. But once the grid appears it seems, I would submit, quite resistant to change. The mature careers of Mondrian or Albers are examples of this. No one would characterize the course of decade after decade of their later work as developmental. But by depriving their world of development, one is obviously not depriving it of quality. There is no necessary connection between good art and change, no matter how conditioned we may be to think that there is. Indeed, as we have a more and more extended experience of the grid, we have discovered that one of the most modernist things about it is its capacity to serve as a paradigm or model for the anti-developmental, the anti-narrative, the anti-historical.

This has occurred in the temporal as well as the visual arts—in music, for example, and in dance. It is no surprise then, that as we contemplate this subject, there should have been announced for next season a performance project based on the combined efforts of Phil Glass, Lucinda Childs, and Sol LeWitt: music, dance, and sculpture, projected as the mutually accessible space of the grid.

First published in *Grids: Format and Image in 20th Century Art* (New York: The Pace Gallery, 1978)

1 Success here refers to three things at once: a sheerly quantitative success, involving the number of artists in this century who have used grids; a qualitative success through which the grid has become the medium for some of the greatest works of modernism; and an ideological success, in that the grid is able—in a work of whatever quality—to emblematicize the Modern.

2 See Claude Lévi-Strauss, *Structural Anthropology* (New York: 1963), particularly "The Structural Analysis of Myth."

3 Michel-Eugène Chevreul, *De la loi du contraste simultané des couleurs*, Paris, 1839, translated into English in 1872; Charles Blanc, *Grammaire des arts du déssin*, Paris, 1867, translated into English in 1879; Ogden N. Rood, *Modern Chromatics*, New York, 1879, translated into French, 1881; Hermann von Helmholtz, *Handbuch der physiologischen Optik*, Leipzig, 1867; Johann Wolfgang von Goethe, Farbenlehre, 1810, translated into English, 1840.

4 See Lorenz Eitner, "The Open Window and the Storm-Tossed Boat: an Essay in the Iconography of Romanticism," *Art Bulletin* XXXVII (December 1955), 281–90.

5 Robert G. Cohn, "Mallarmé's Windows," *Yale French Studies*, no. 54 (1977), 23–31.

6 This literature is far too extensive to be cited here; a representative and excellent example of this discussion is John Elderfield, "Grids," *Artforum* X (May 1972), 52–59.

One has to move back and forth to experience the work. … follow the disappearing and emerging lines in the gesso surface, like veins beneath the skin

fifty two twenty one, 2020 copper wire embedded in gesso panel

fifty two twenty one, 2020 (details)

fifty one twenty one, 2020 copper wire embedded in gesso panel

fifty one twenty one, 2020 (detail)

I/forty four, 2019 thinnam on gesso panels

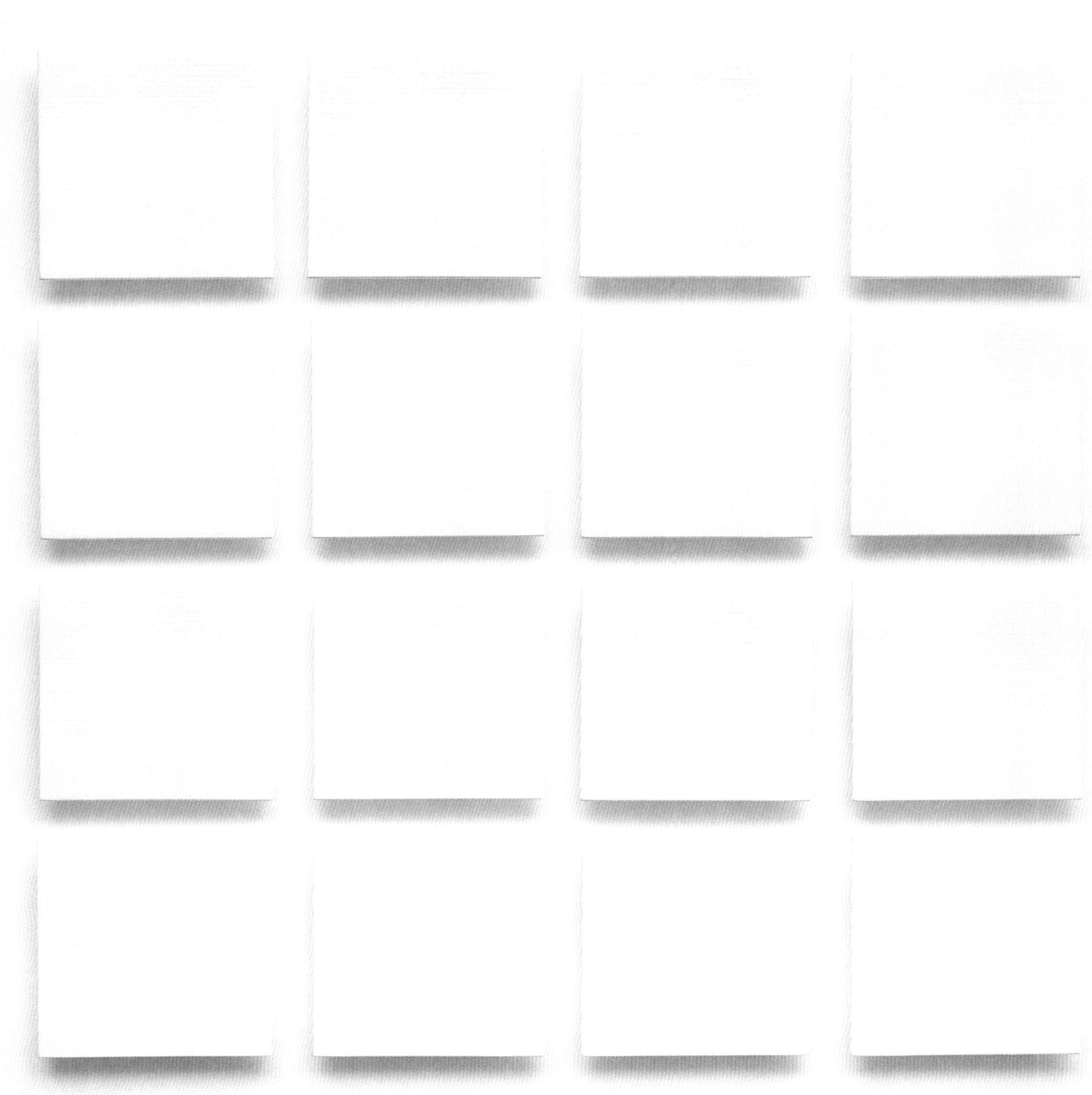

I/forty four, 2019 (details)

I/forty seven, 2018   copper wire embedded in gesso panel   overleaf   (detail)

I/hundred eighteen, 2018 copper wire embedded in gesso panel

I/hundred fifty nine, 2019 thinnam on gesso panel opposite (detail)

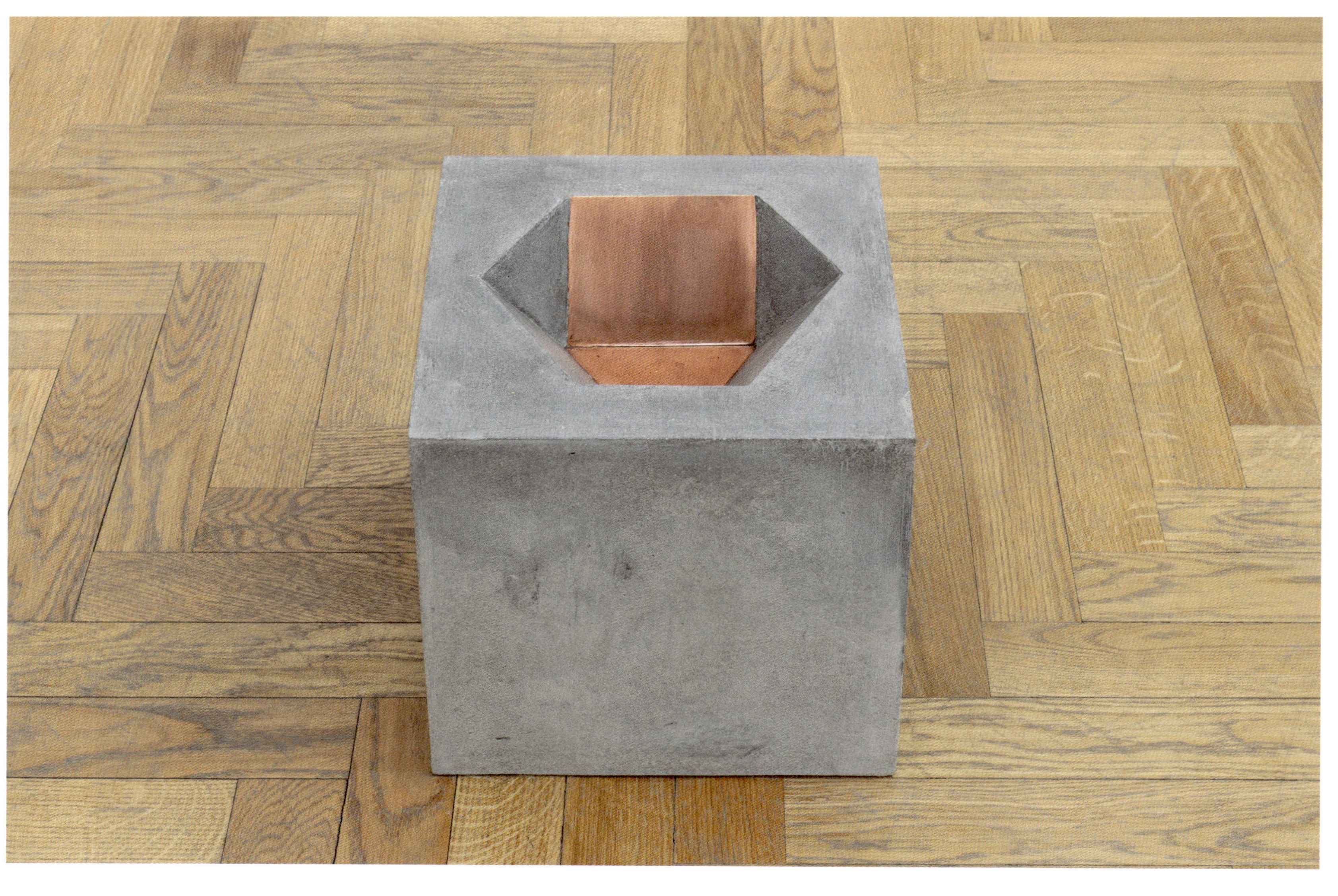

eighteen one zero-0525, 2019 concrete and copper

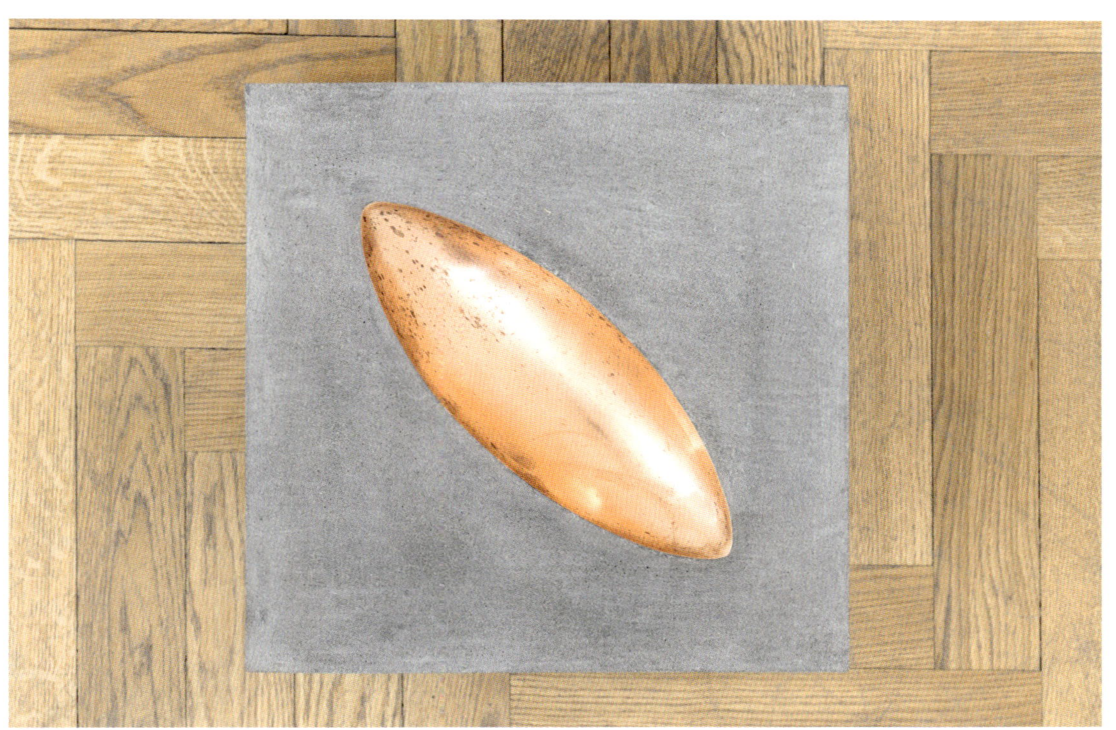

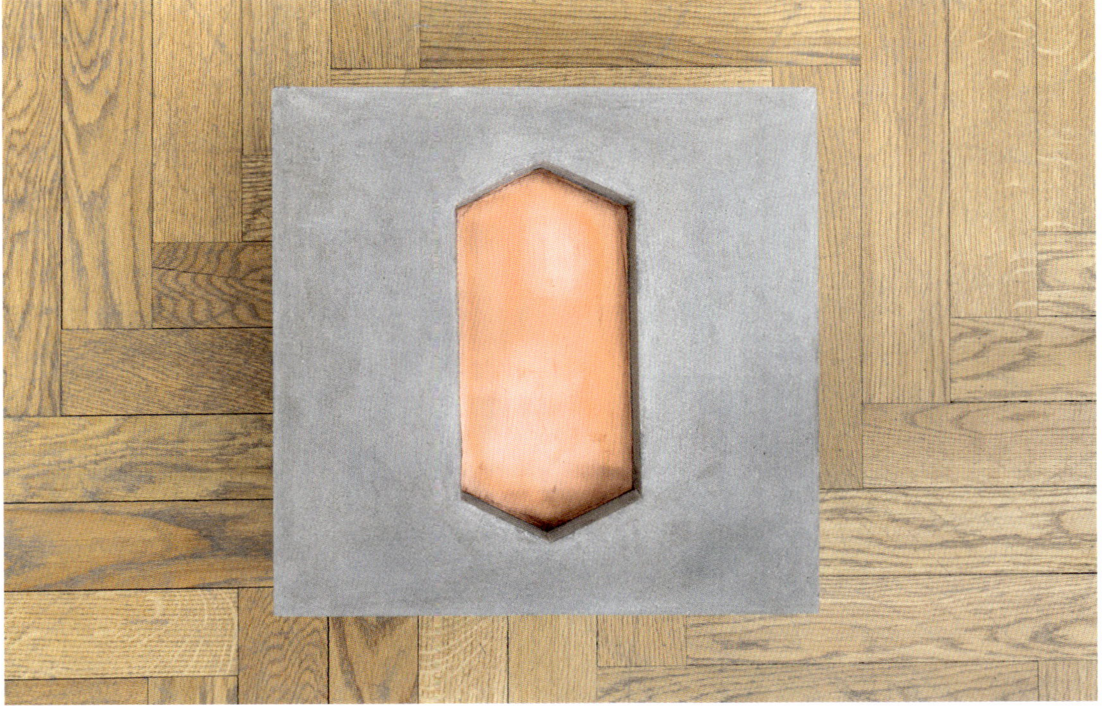

top thirty two five-0645, 2019 concrete and copper bottom fifteen six zero-0630, 2019 concrete and copper

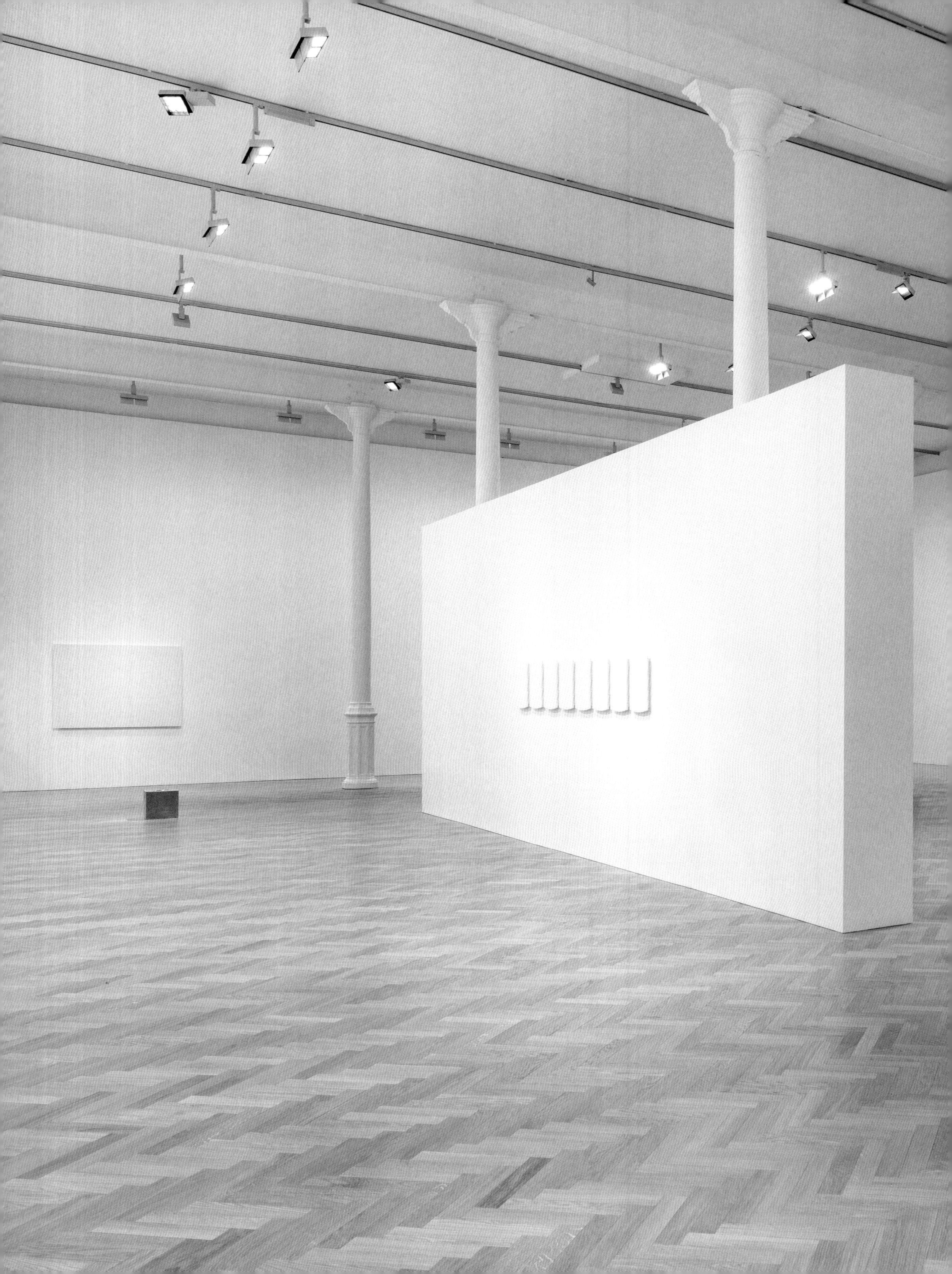

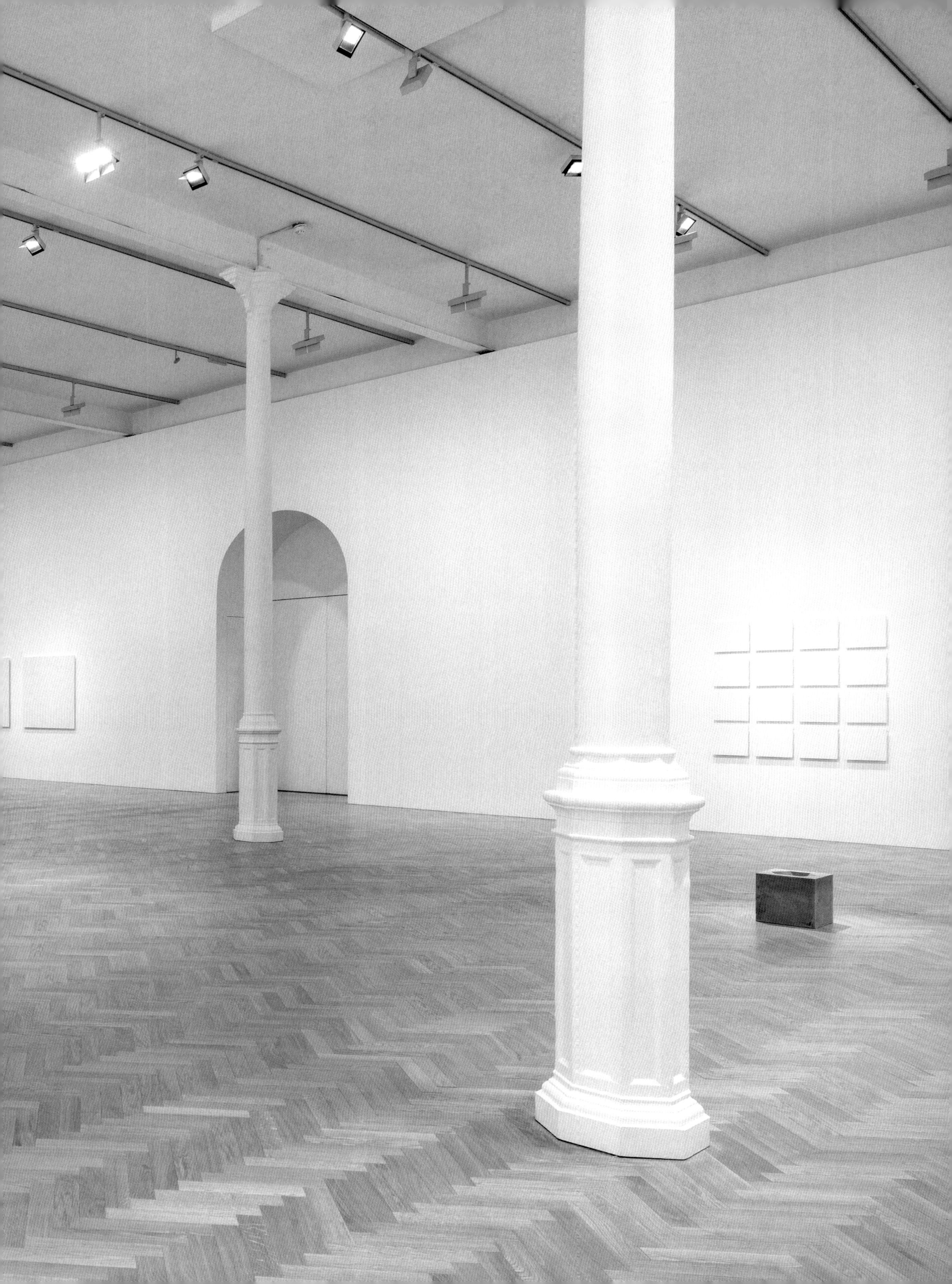

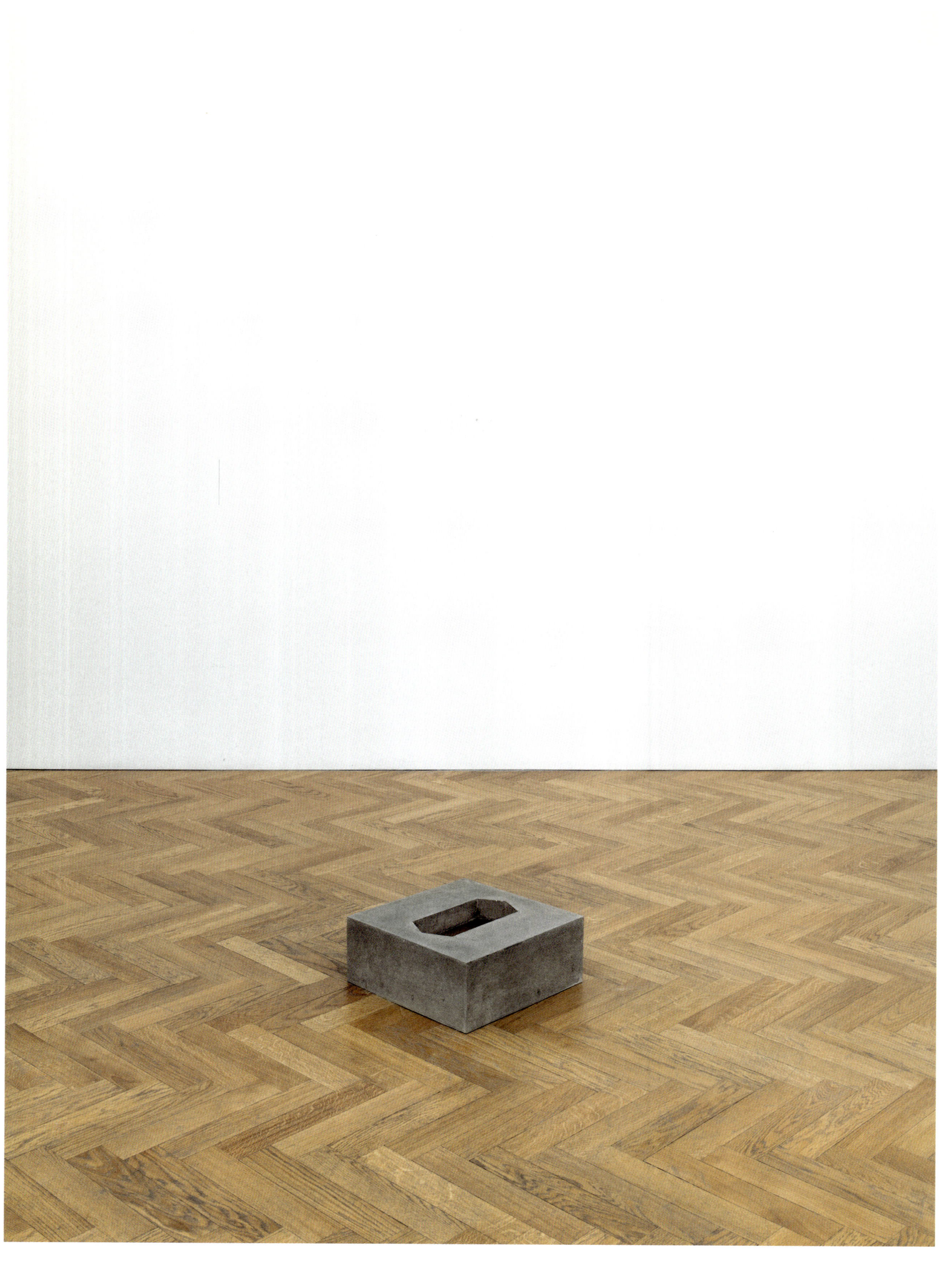

previous installation view Pace Gallery, London, 2019 above fifteen six zero-0630, 2019 concrete and copper

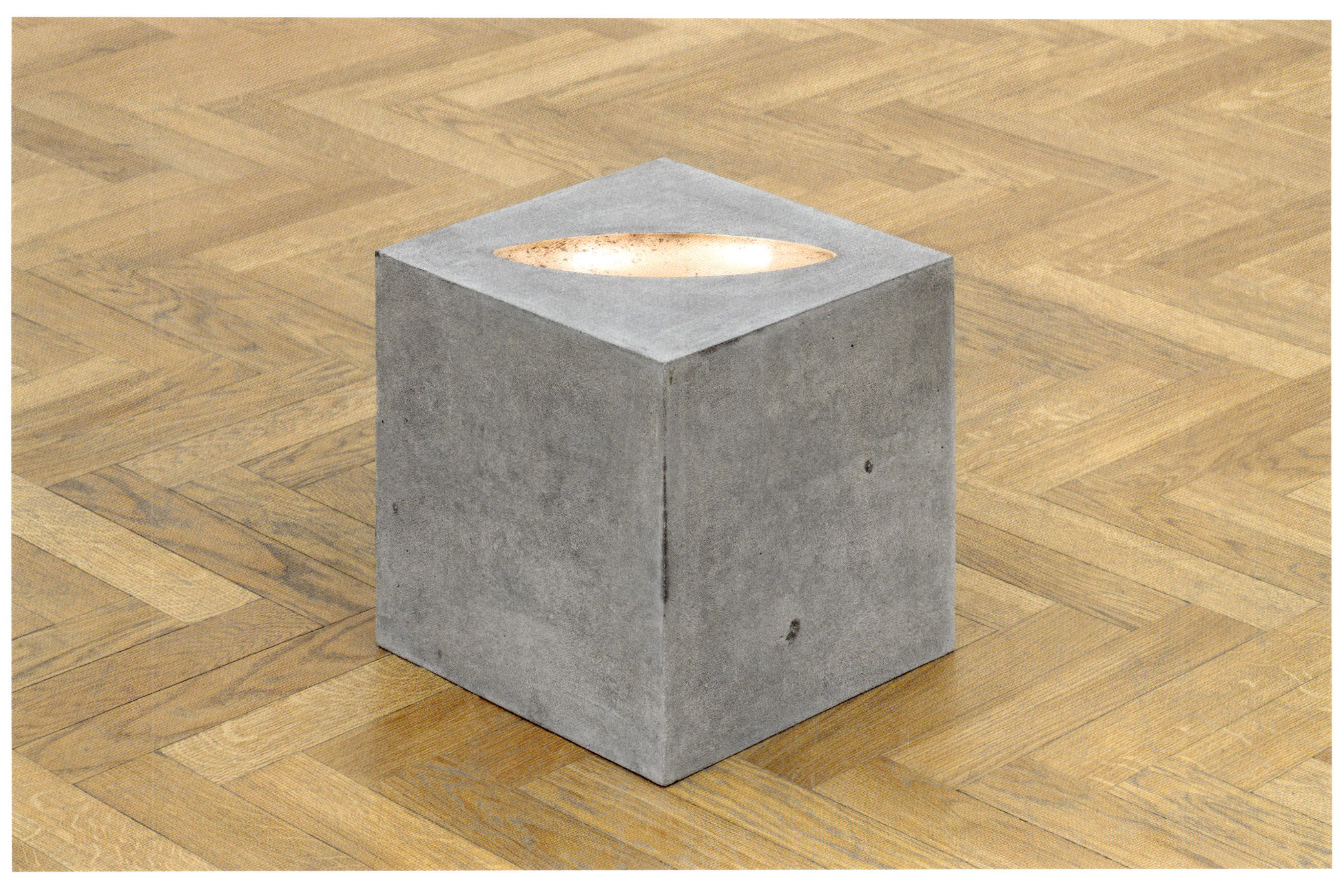

thirty two five-0645, 2019 concrete and copper

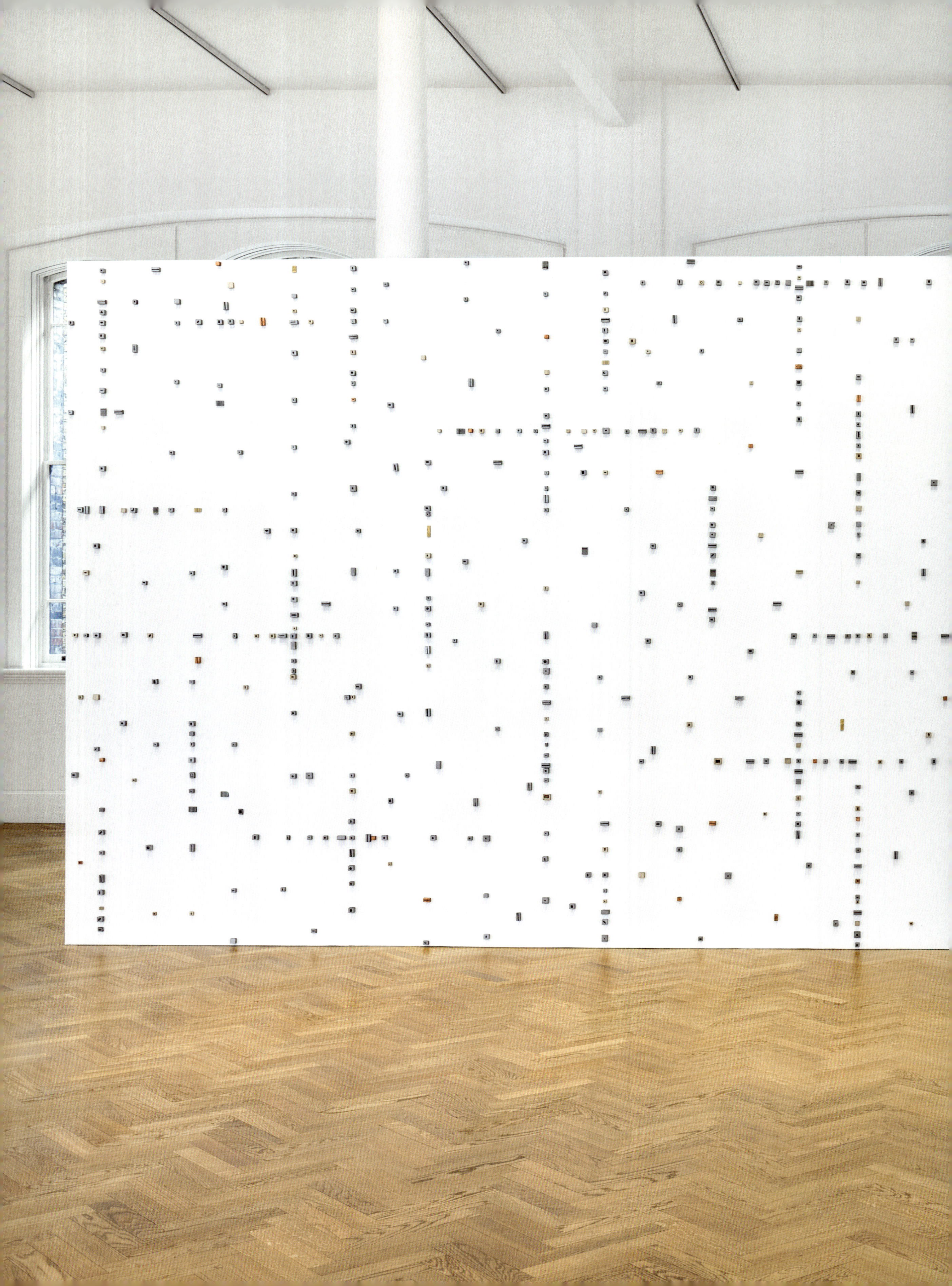

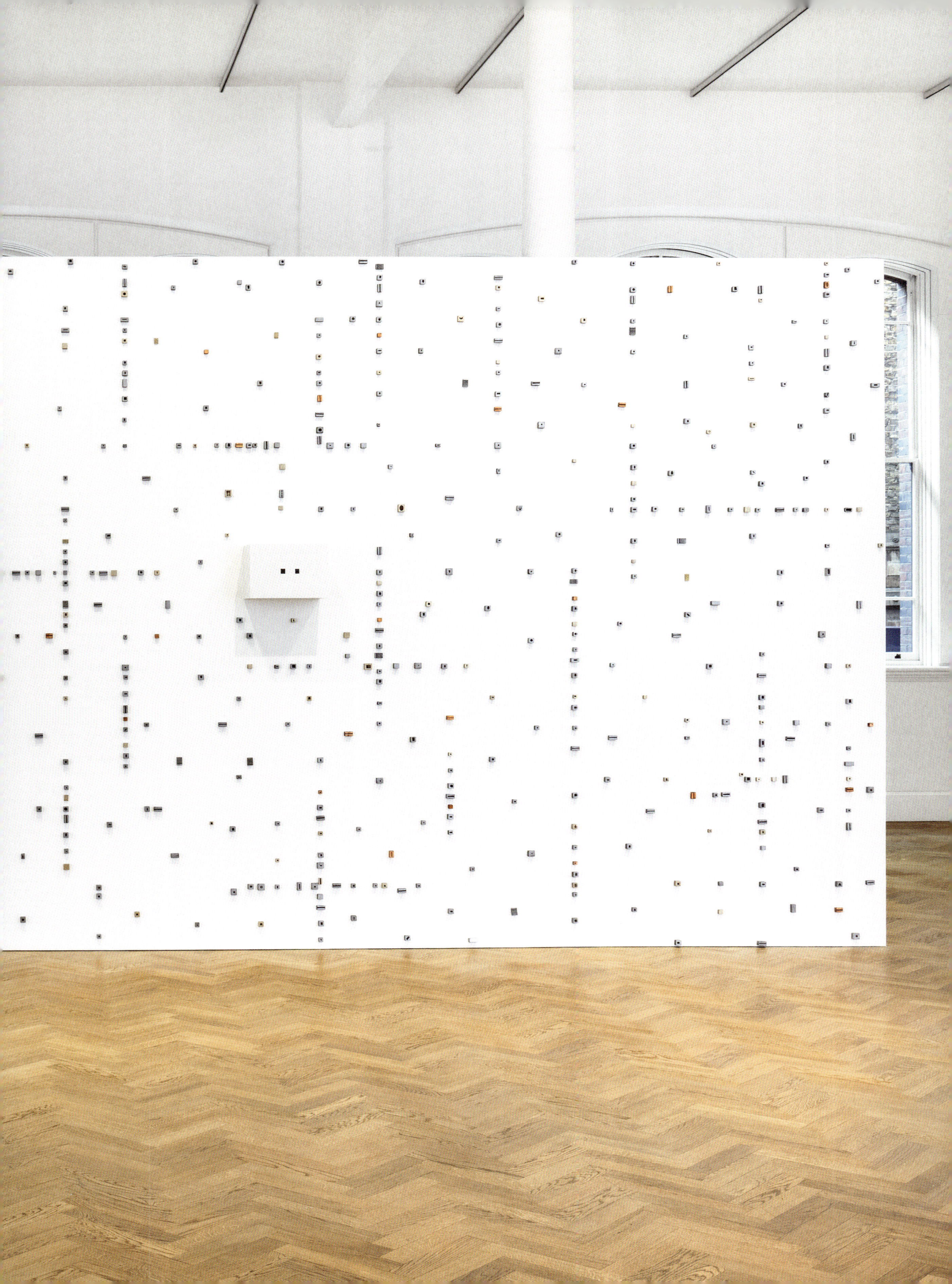

previous installation view Pace Gallery, London, 2019 sb/eighteen, 2018 found objects (iron, copper, and brass) and gesso opposite (detail)

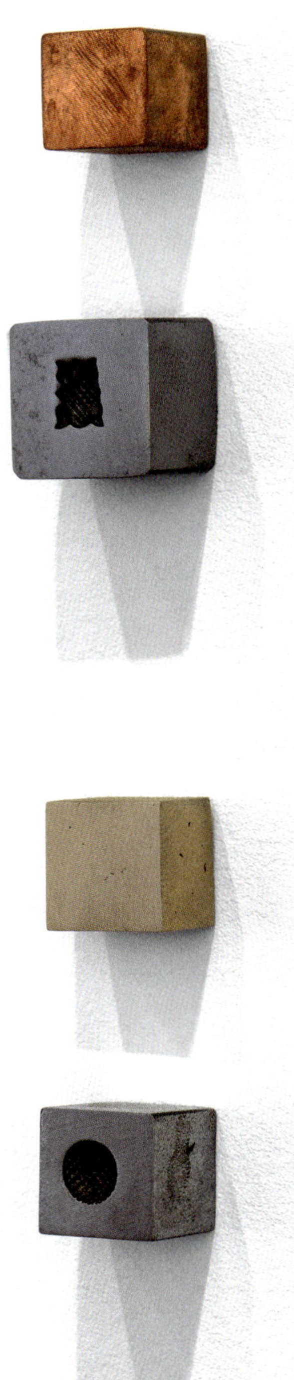

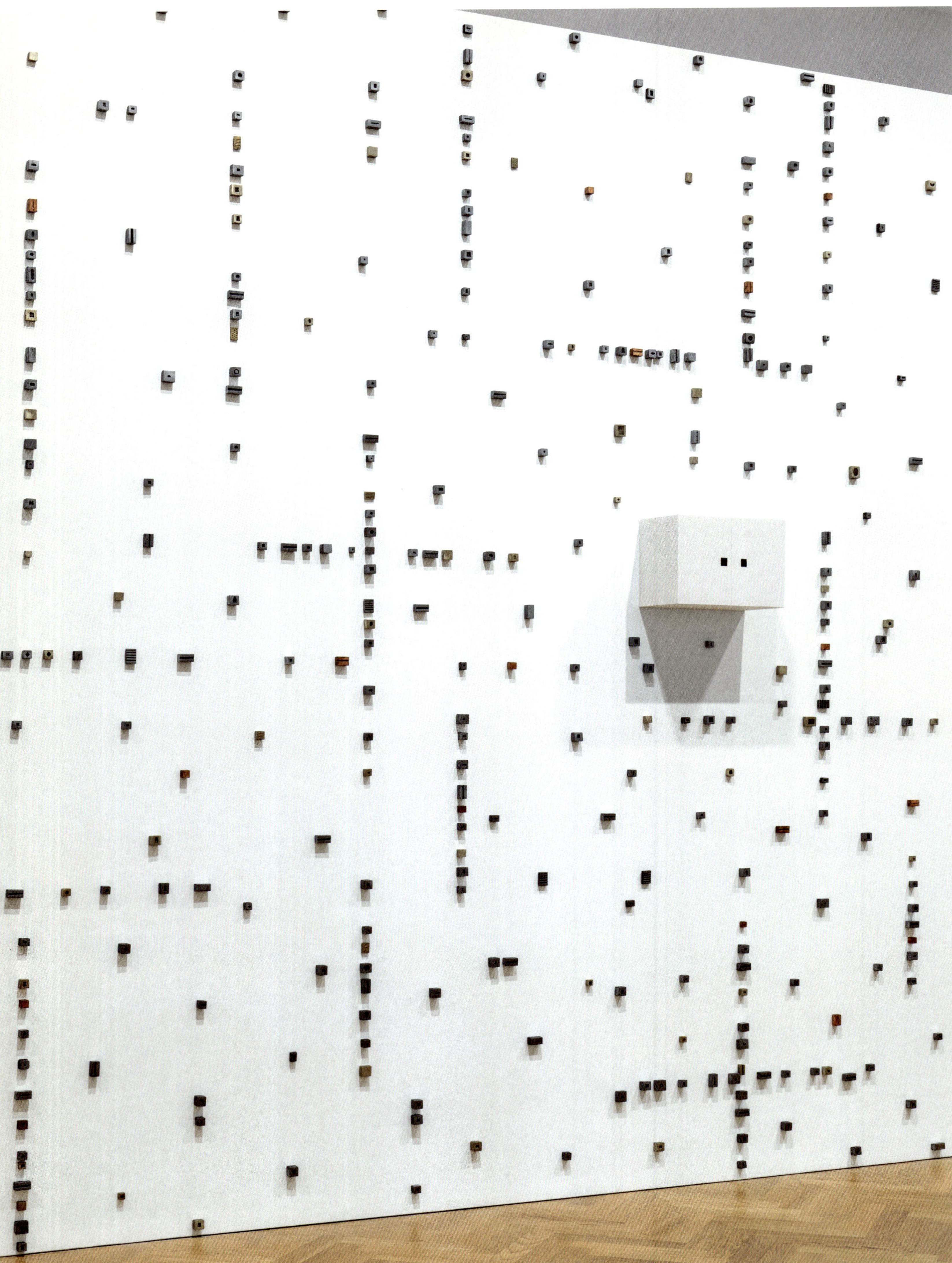

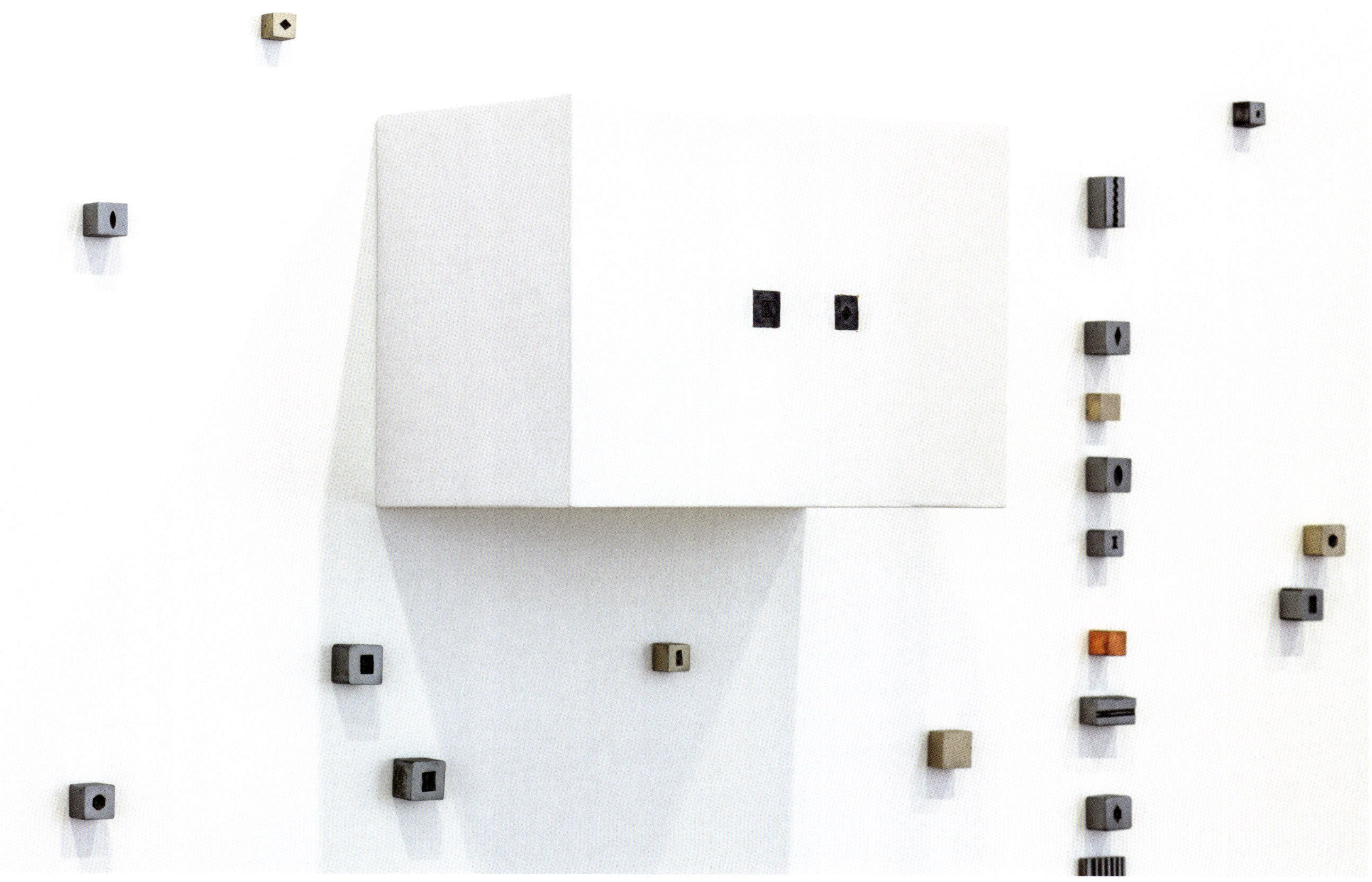

sb/eighteen, 2018 (details)

I/hundred ninety four, 2018 copper wire embedded in gesso panel overleaf (detail)

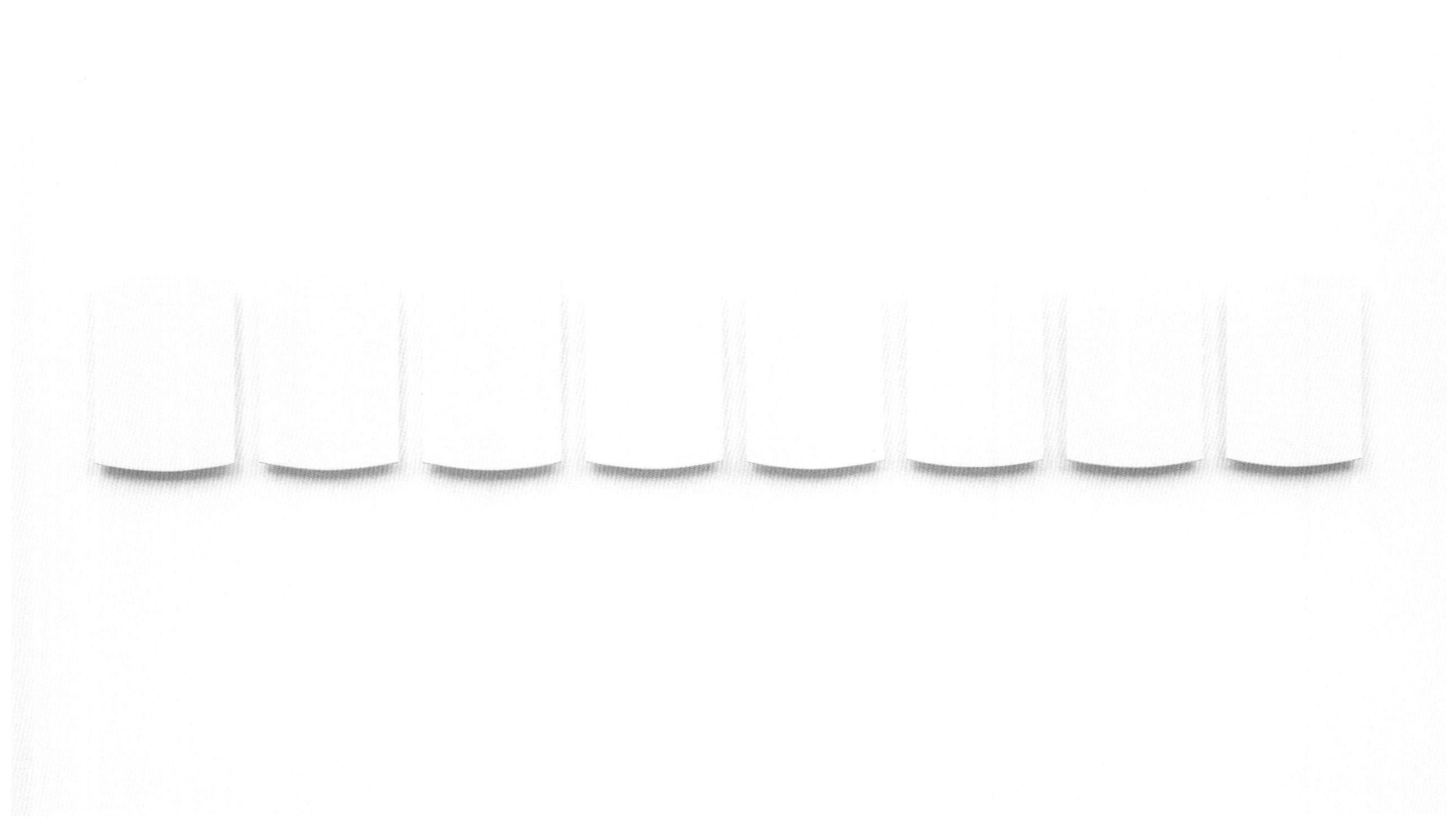

I/hundred fifty eight, 2019 thinnam on gesso panels opposite (detail)

forty three nineteen, 2019 thinnam on gesso panel

forty three nineteen, 2019 (detail)

I/hundred thirty seven, 2019 thinnam on gesso panels

I/hundred thirty seven, 2019 (detail)

The object-like quality of the panel inspired me to push the boundaries further—to explore how a finely made gesso panel… was more than just a surface for painting

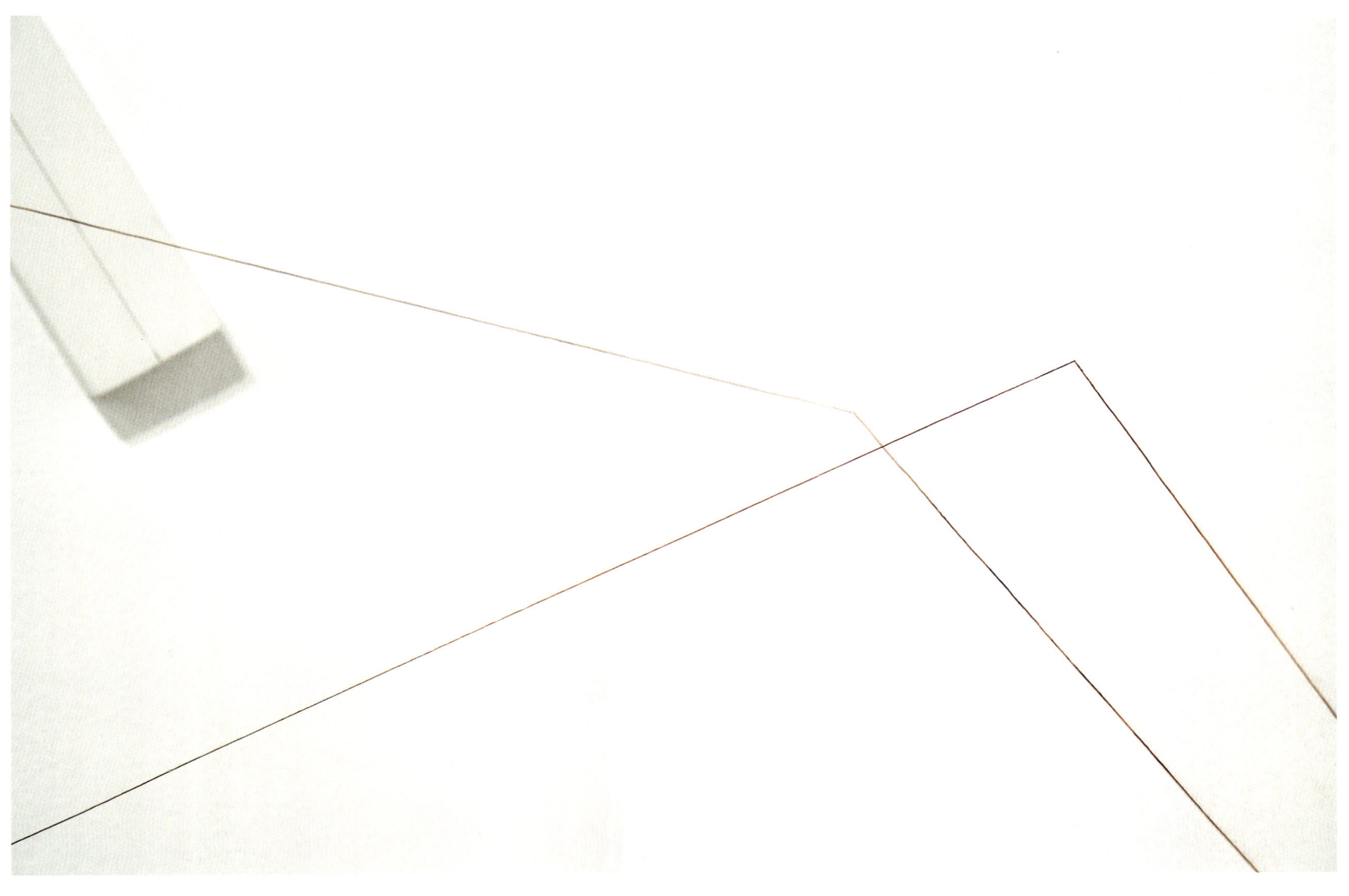

overleaf installation view Dhaka Art Summit, 2020 dp/twenty/thirteen, 2019 copper wire and copper wire embedded in gesso panel above (detail)

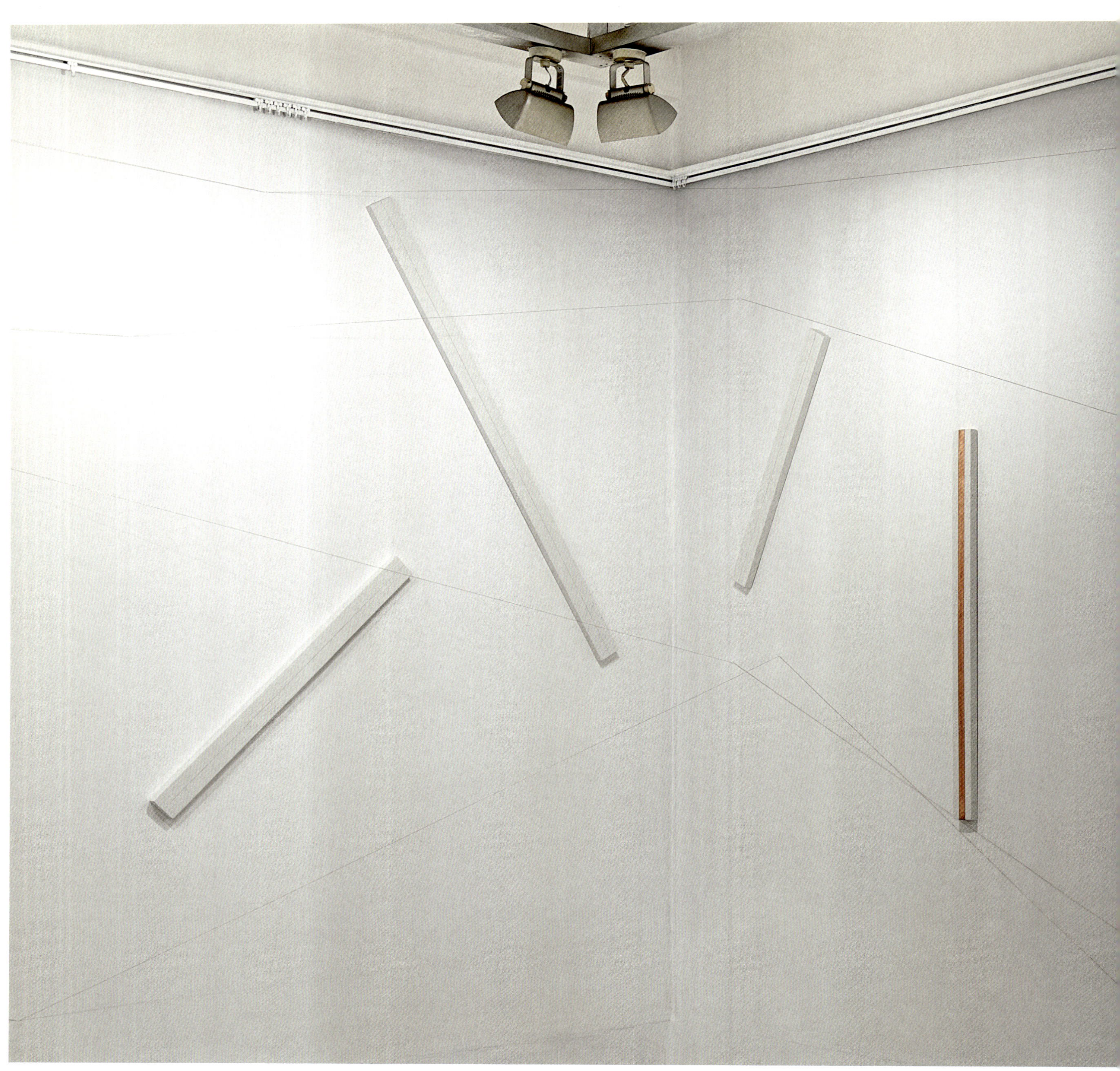

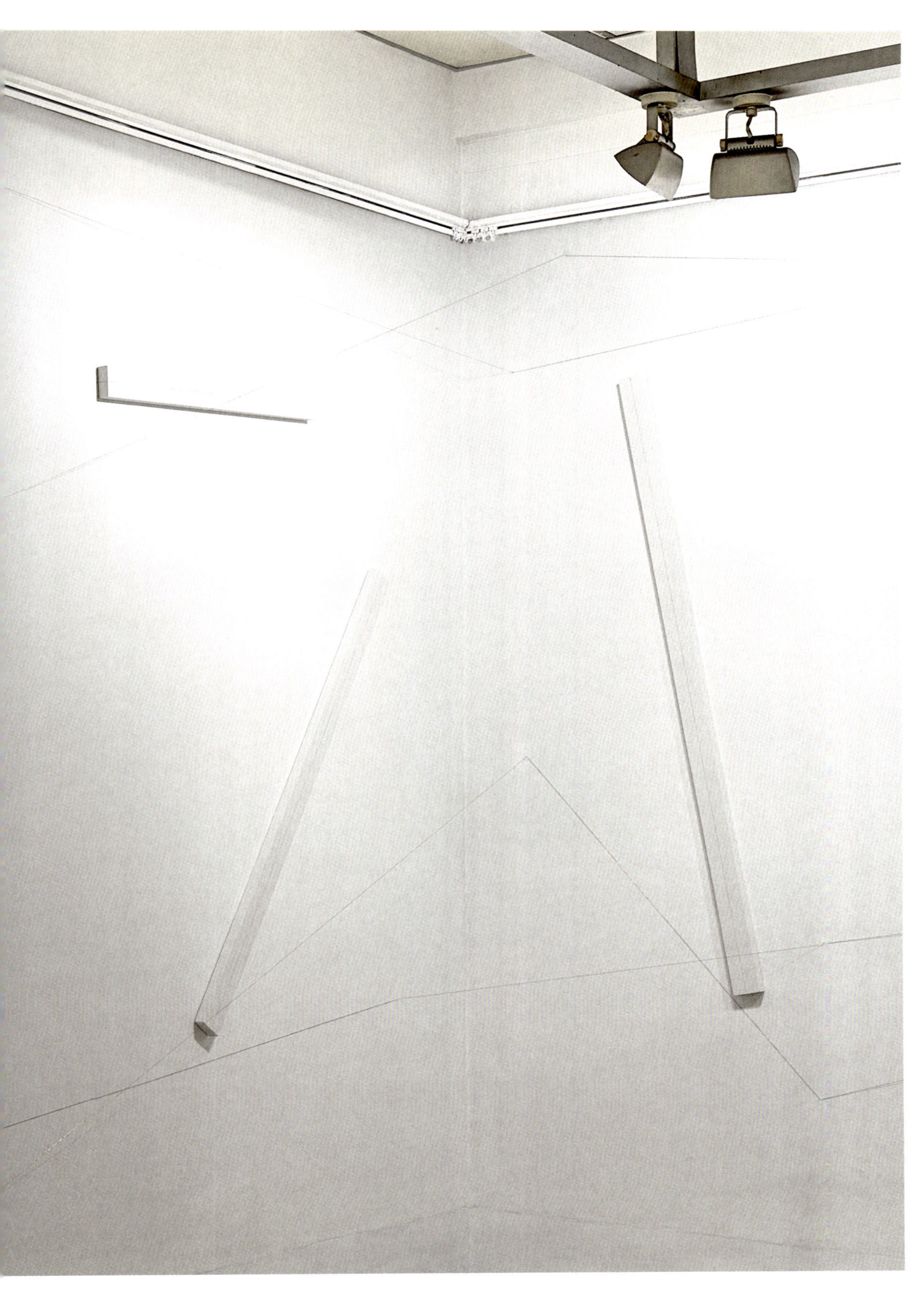

dp/twenty/six, 2019 thinnam on gesso panel

dp/twenty/six, 2019 (details)

dp/twenty/forty eight, 2019 wood, gesso, and copper

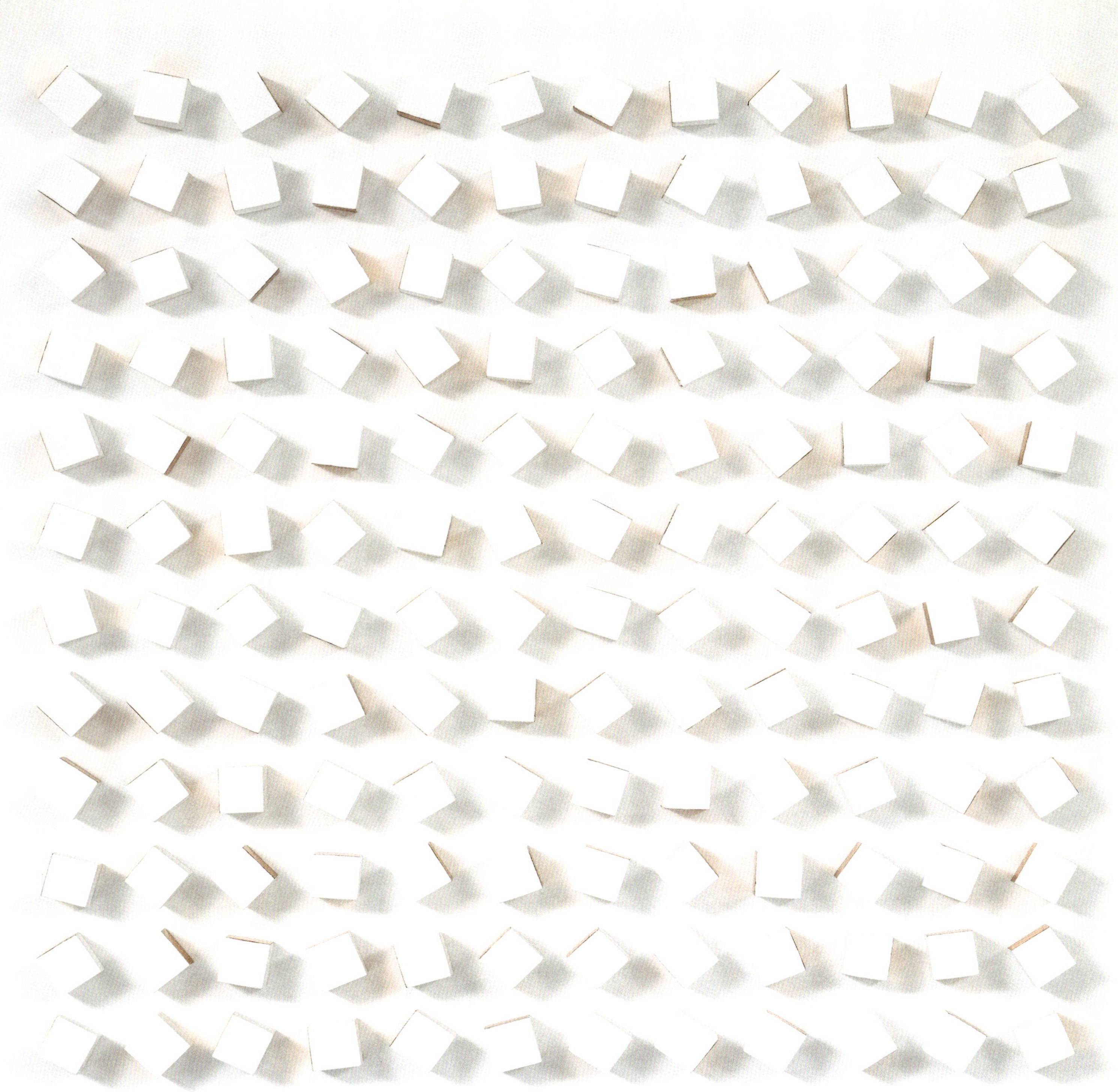

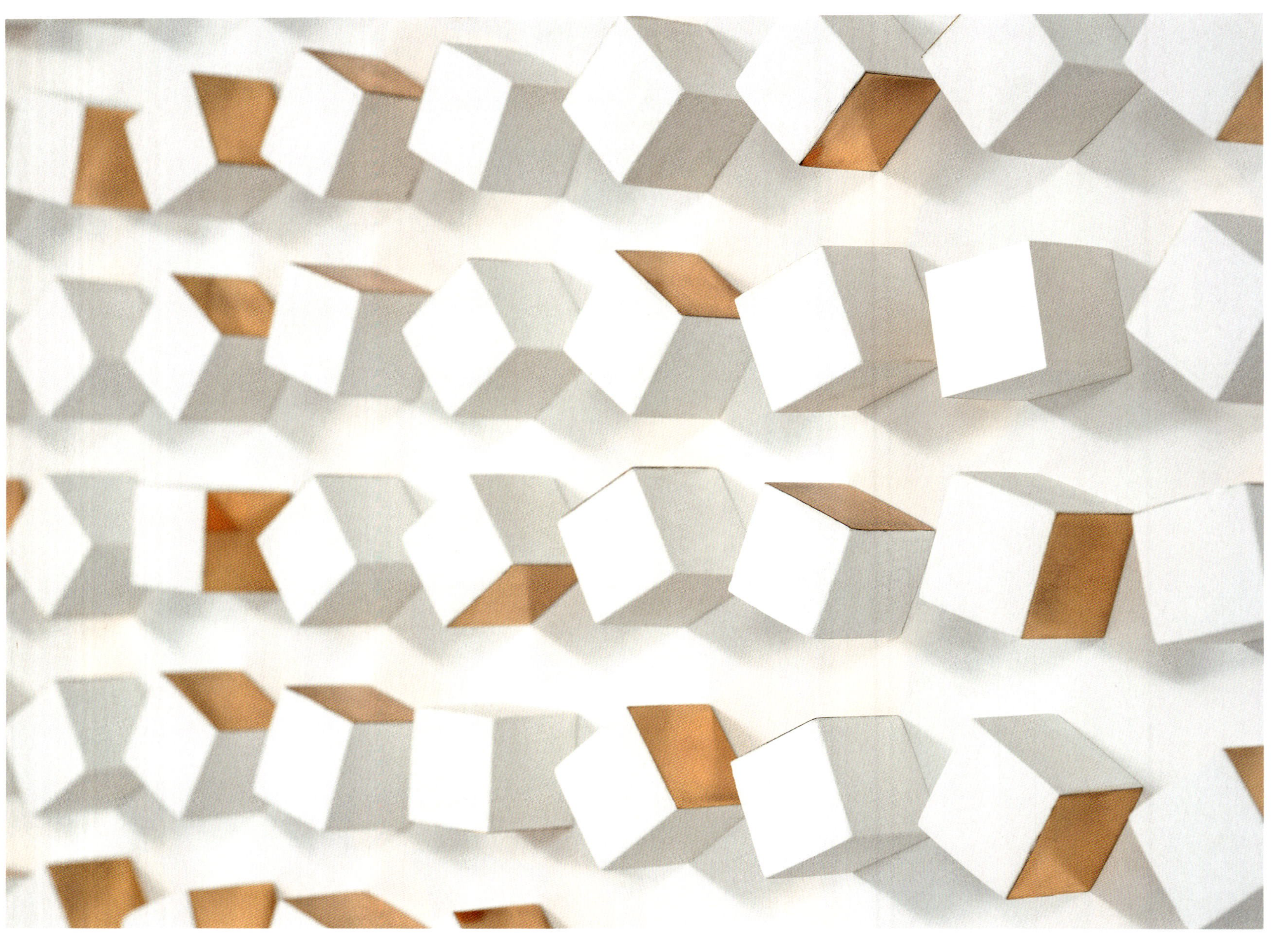

dp/twenty/forty eight, 2019 (detail)

forty five nineteen, 2019 thinnam on gesso panels

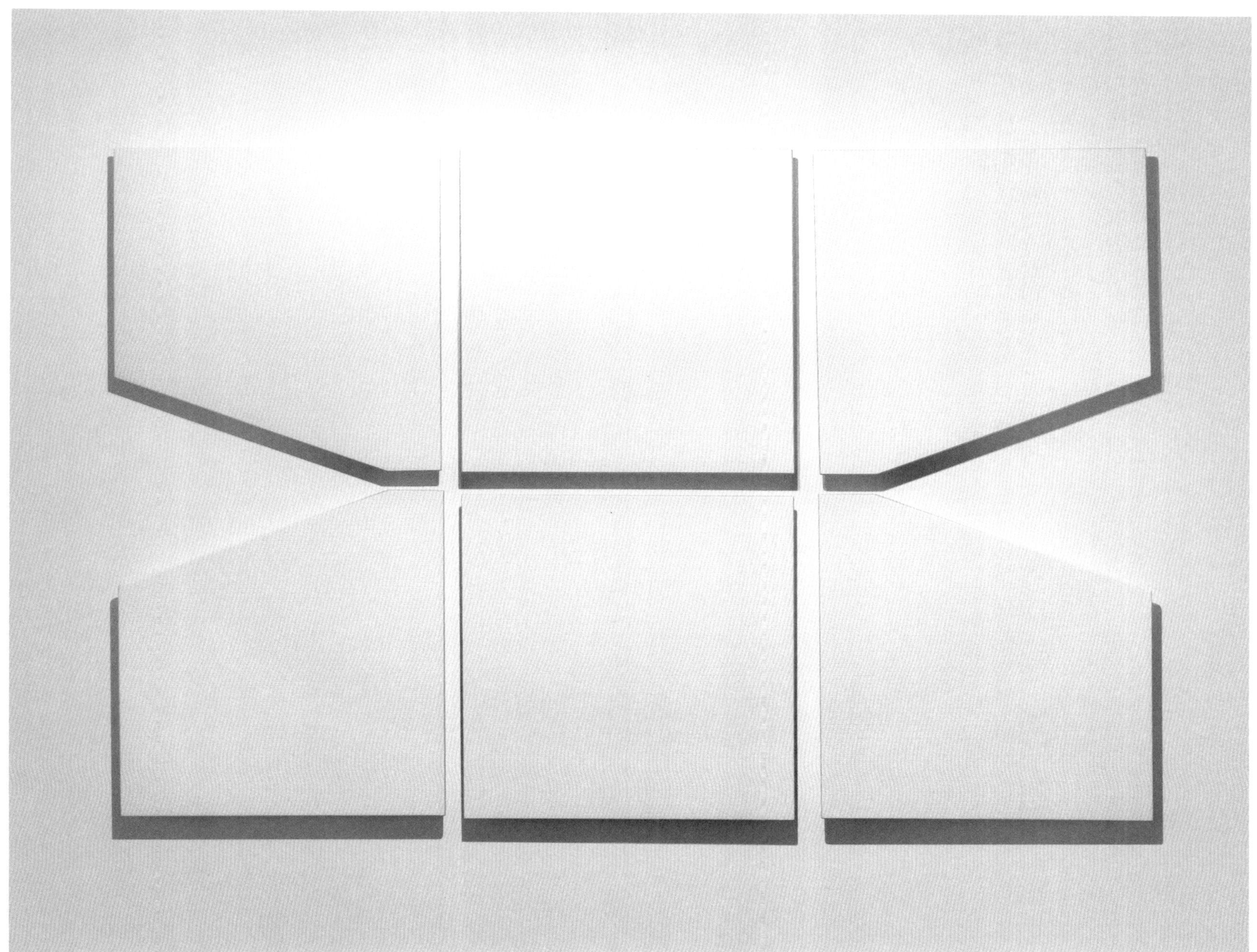

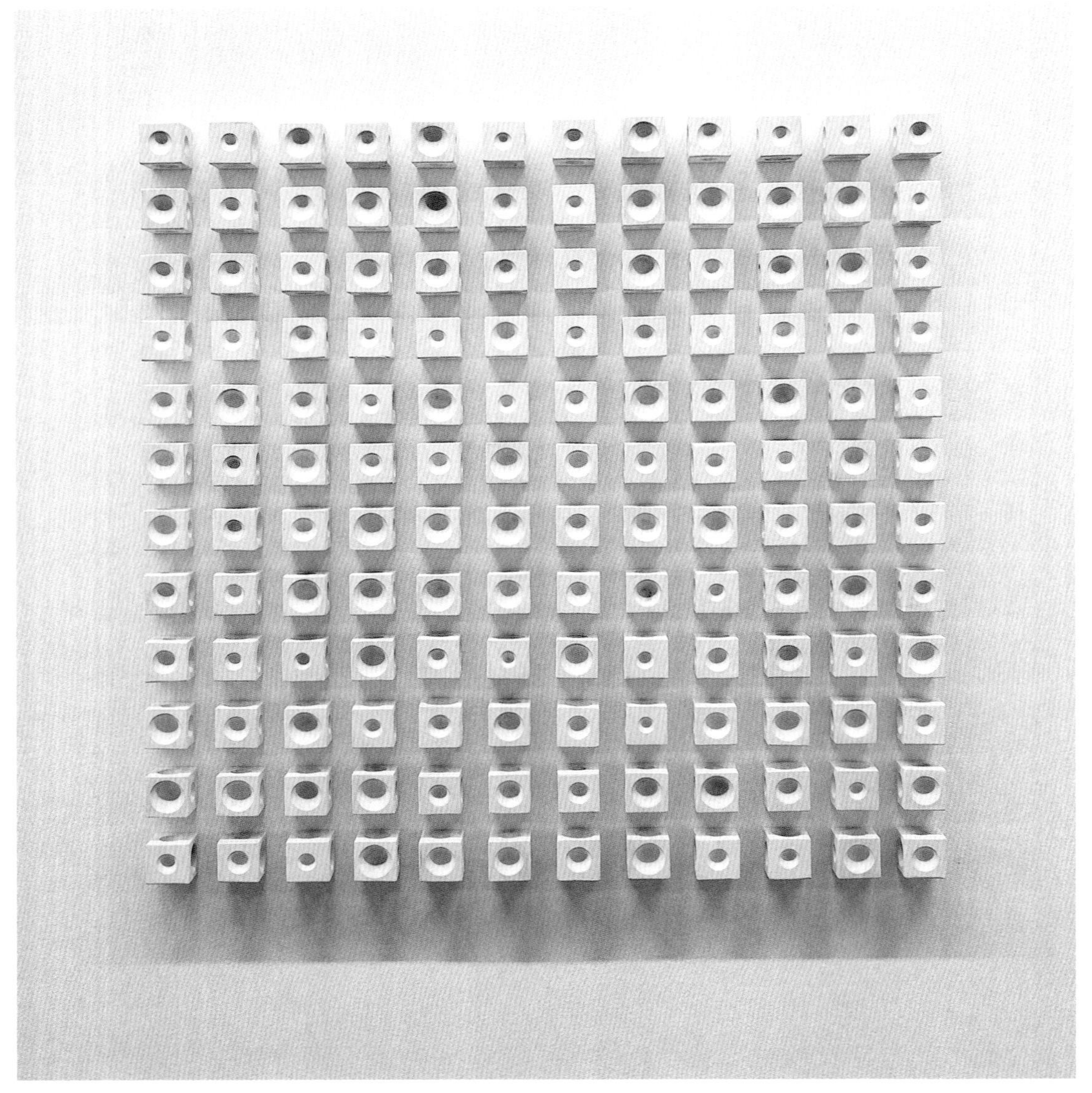

d sixty four, 2017 gesso on found objects opposite (detail)

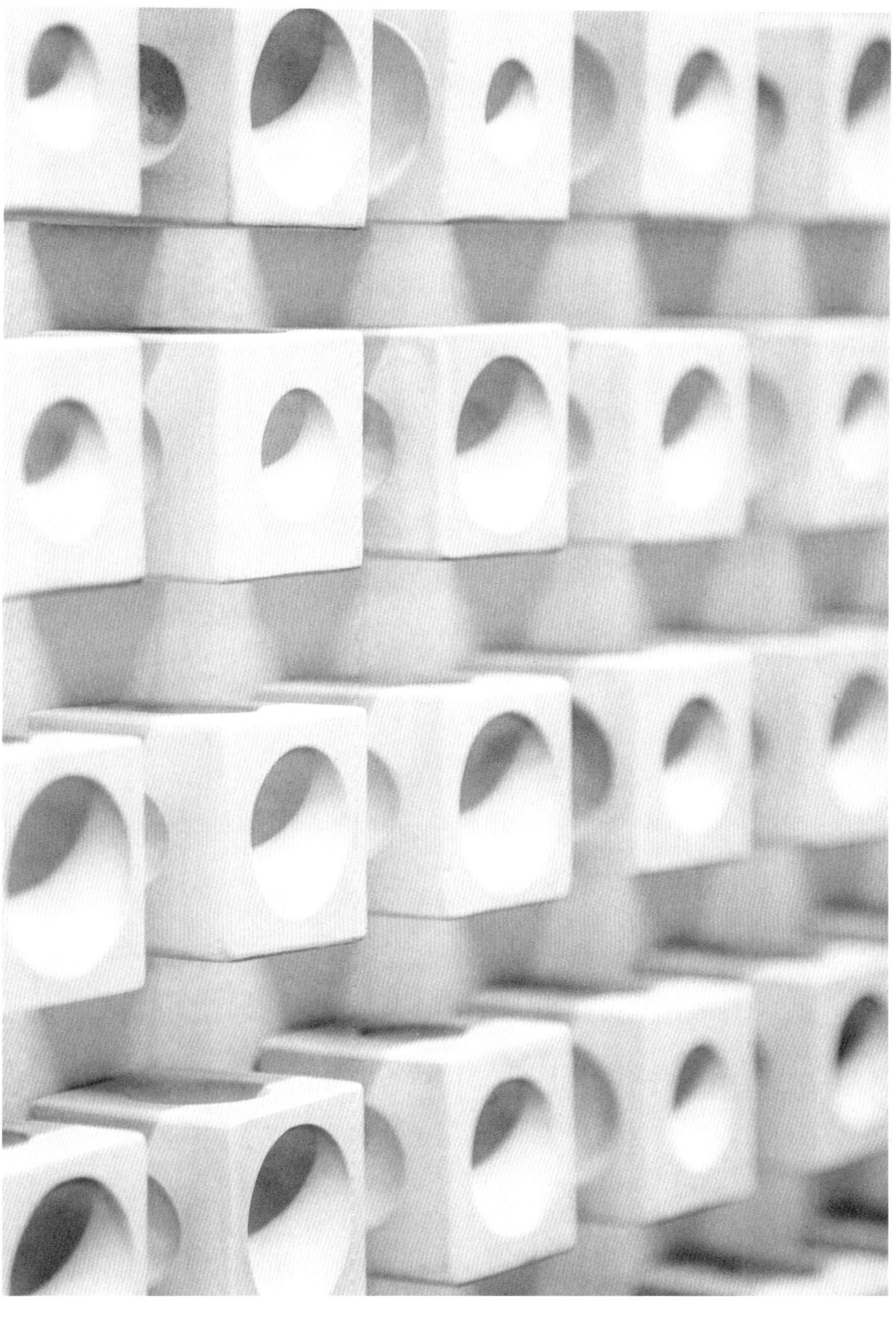

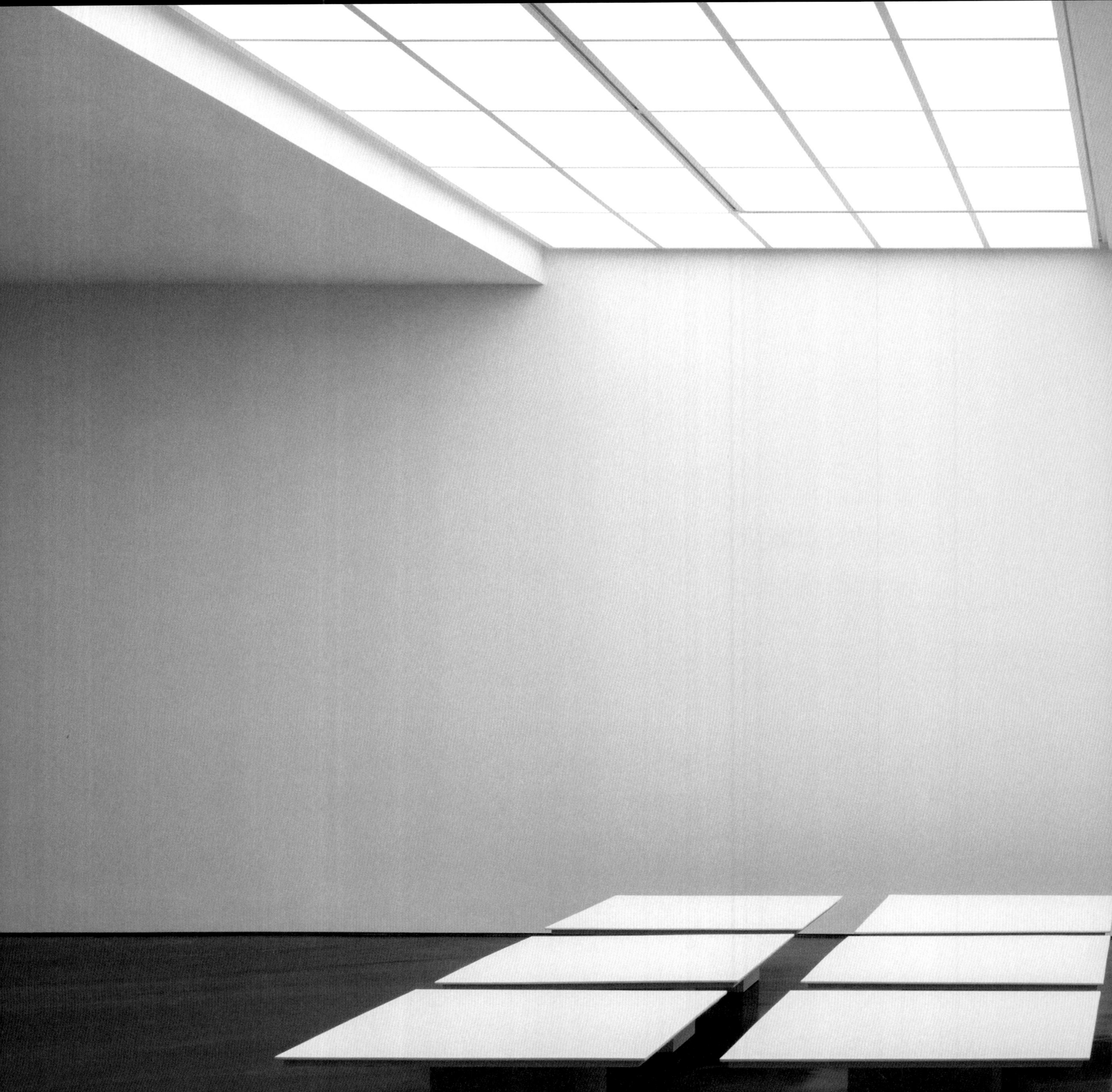

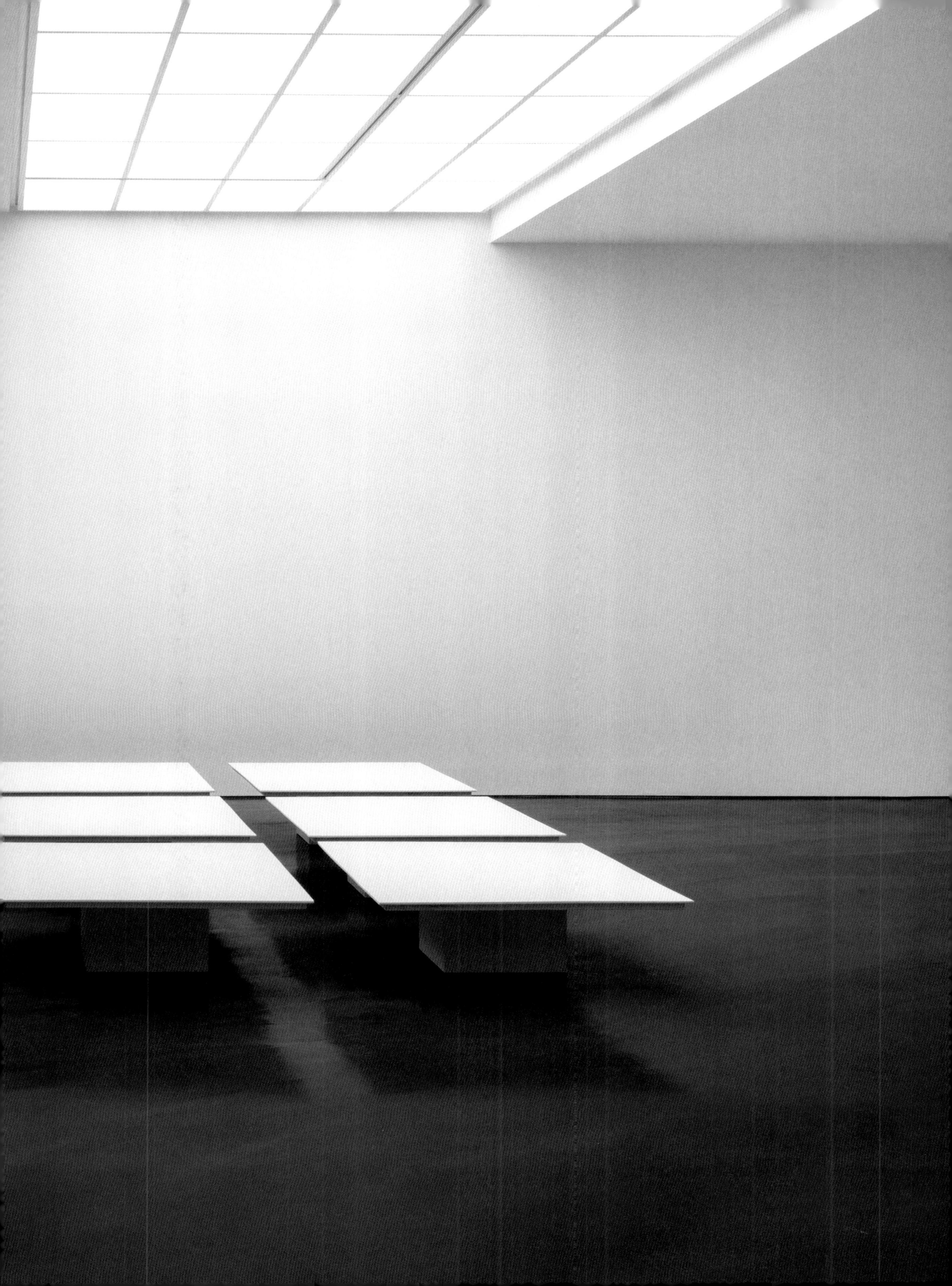

previous installation view Esther Schipper, Berlin, 2018 se/one half, 2017–18 copper wire embedded in gesso panels opposite (detail)

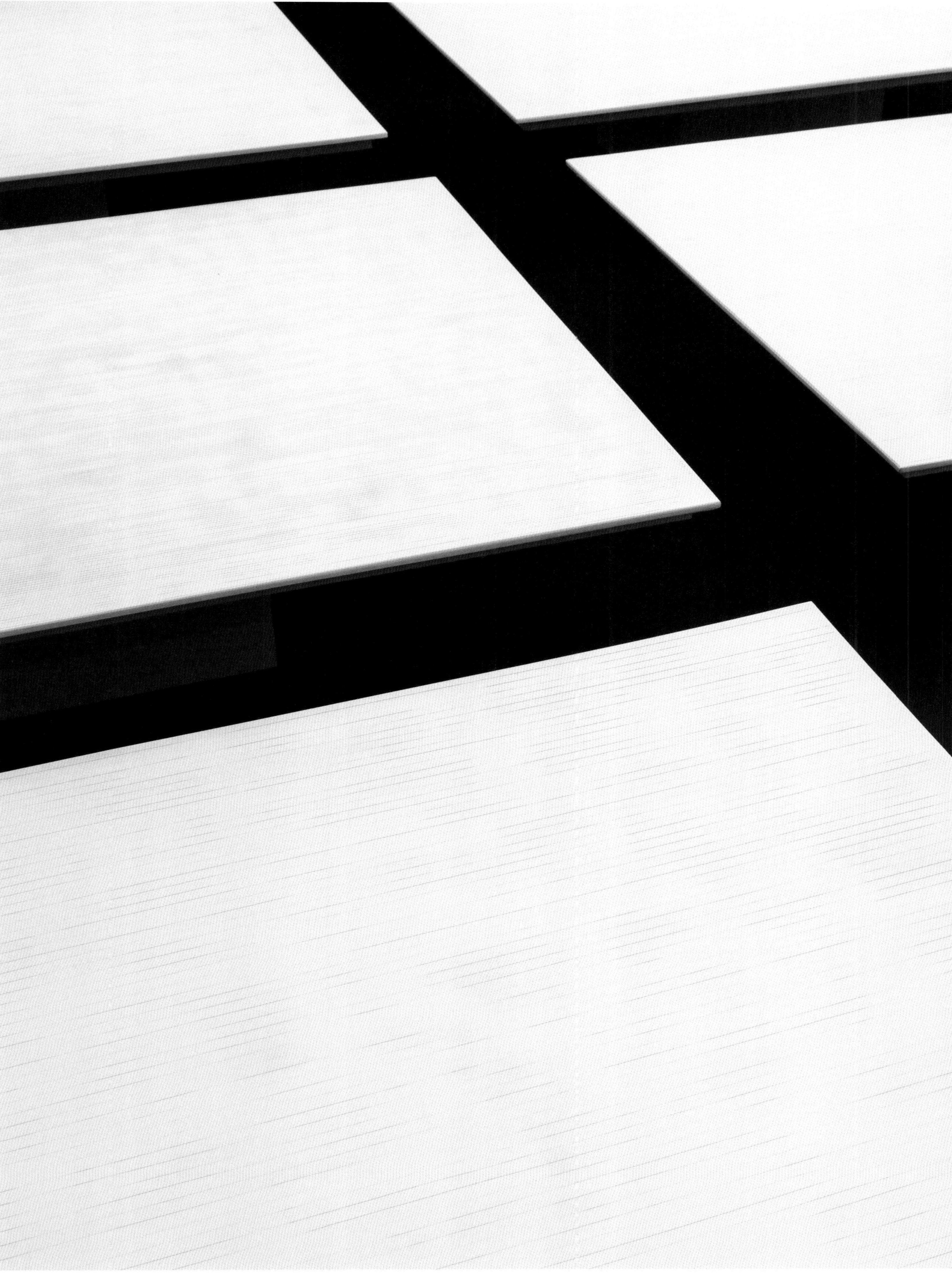

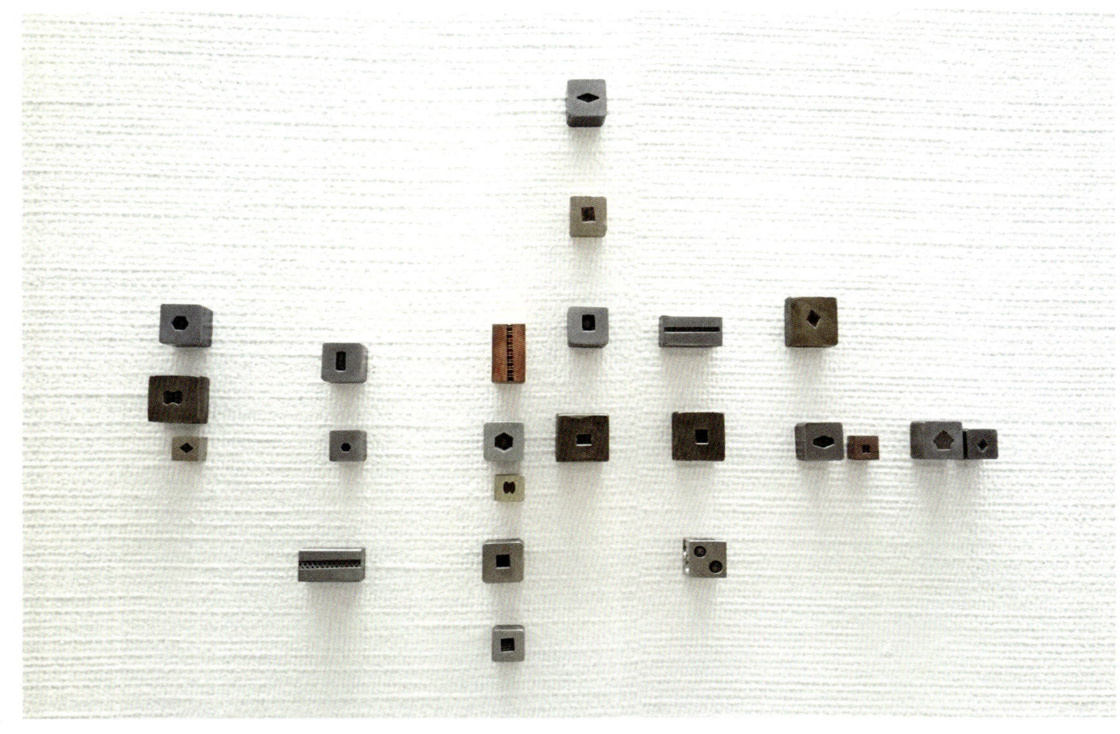

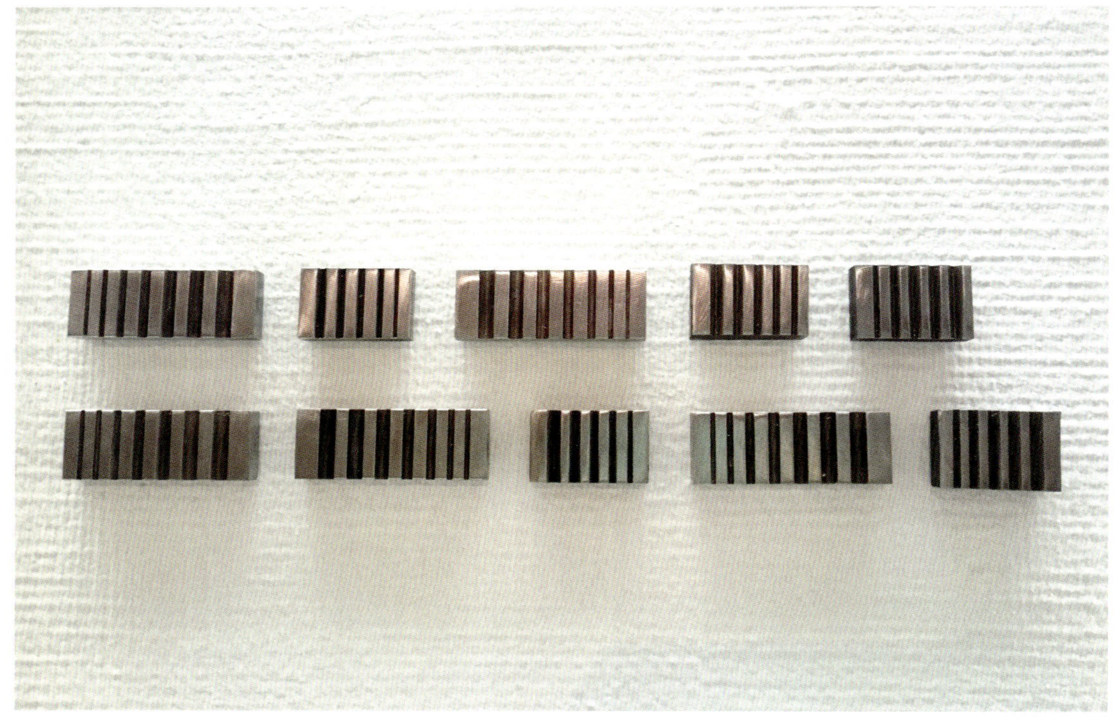

yt/twenty five, 2017 found objects (iron, copper, and brass) (details)

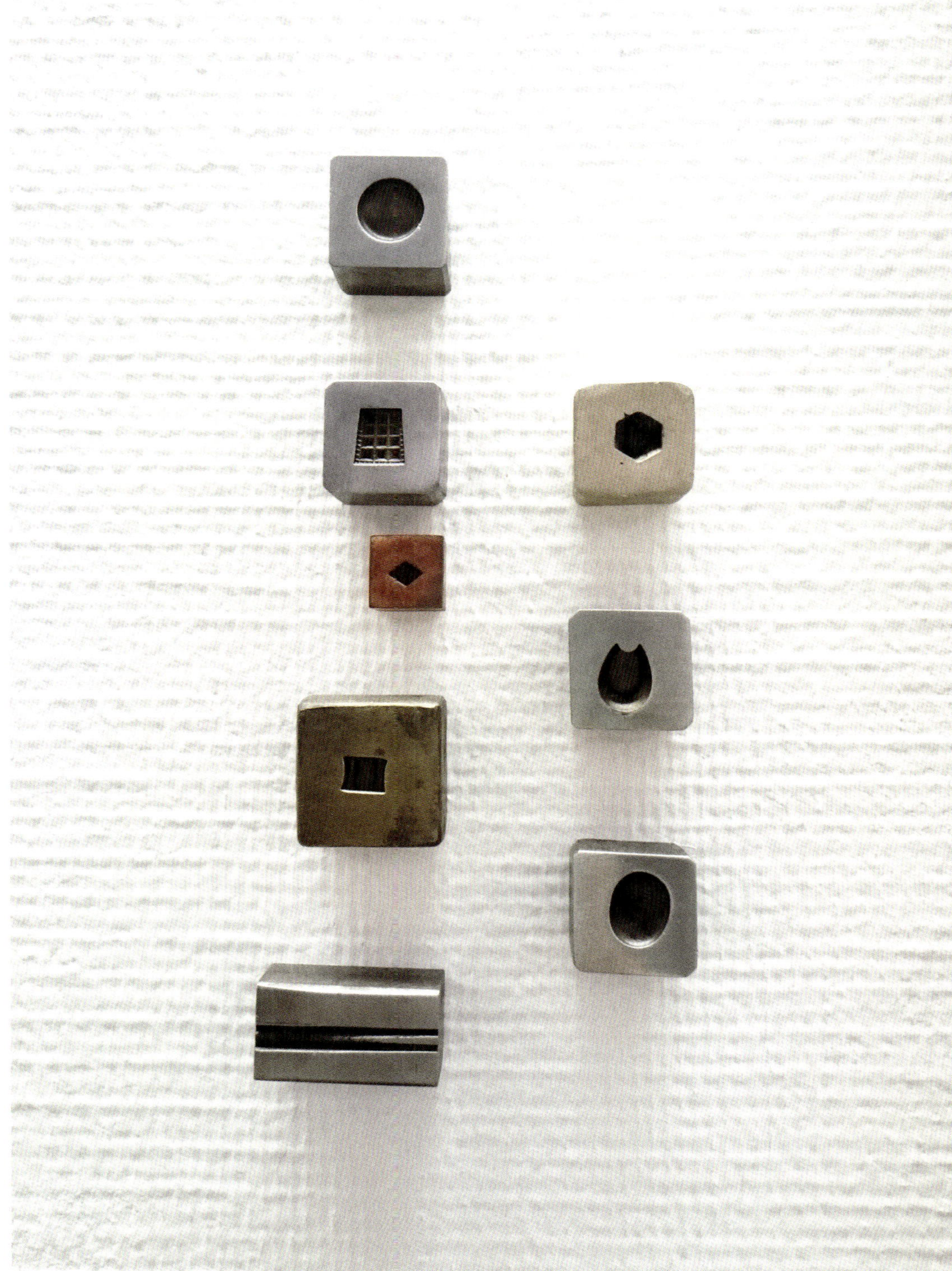

installation view Yokohama Triennale, 2017 yt/forty two, 2017 copper wire and hook screws

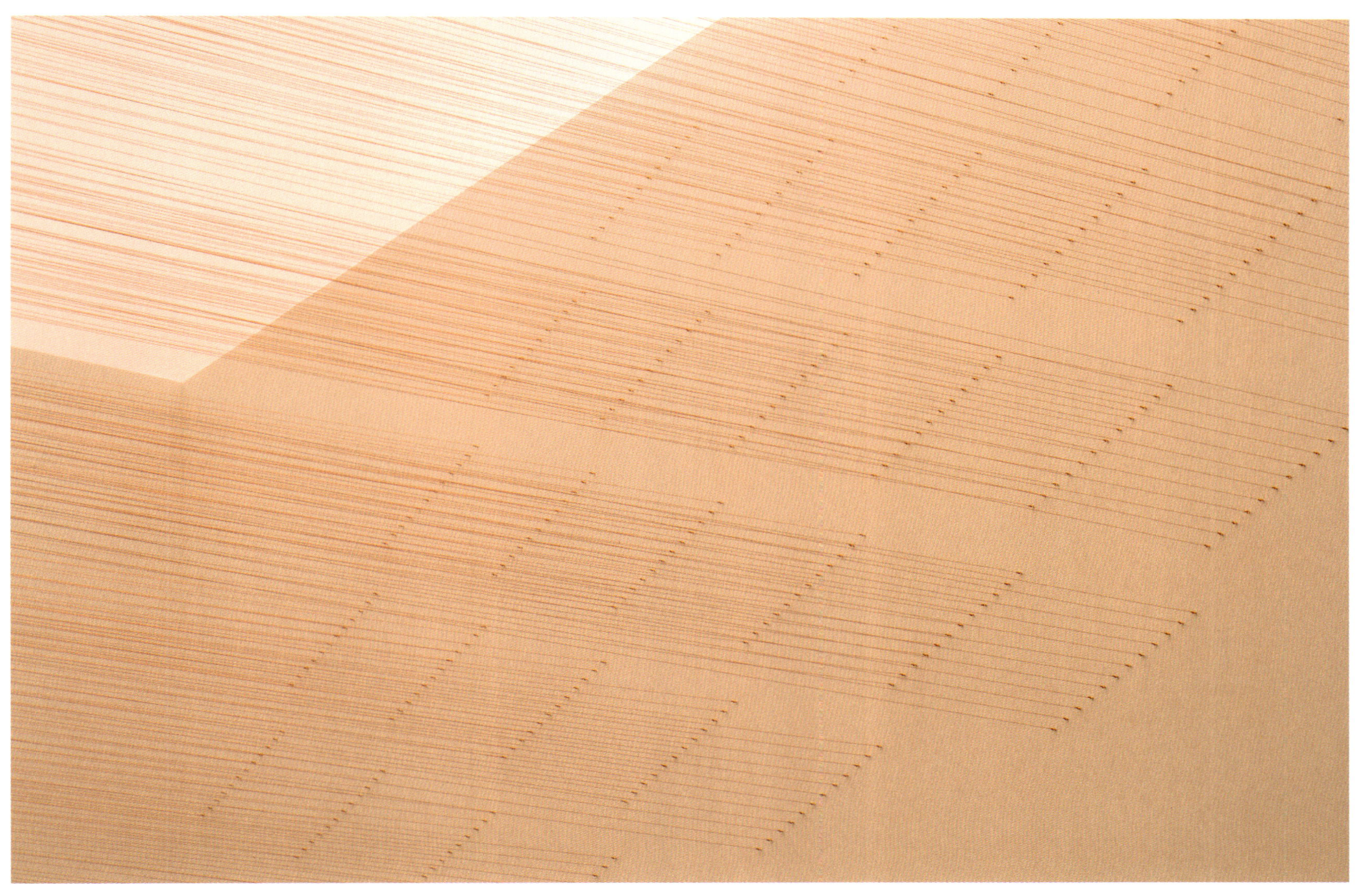

installation view Yokohama Triennale, 2017 yt/forty two, 2017 copper wire and hook screws

installation view   Drawing Room, London, 2017

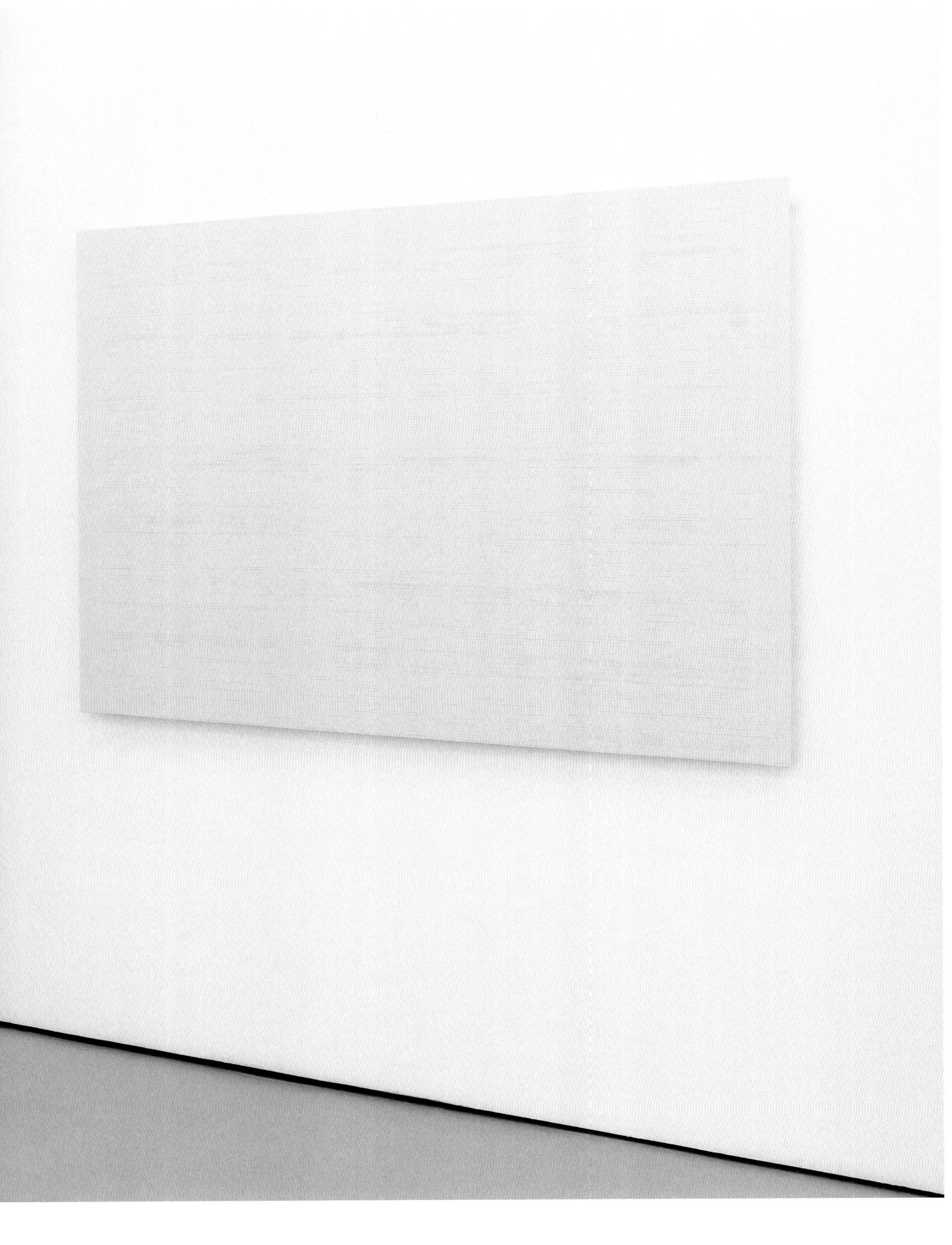

twenty six seventeen, 2017 copper wire embedded in gesso panel

Surface Echoes

Mami Kataoka

Nāgārjuna, a high priest in India who was active during the second and third centuries, contributed to the systematization of Mahāyāna and Esoteric Buddhism. He is also known as the founder of the Mādhyamika school, and in his main work, *Mūlamadhyamakakārikā (Verses on the Middle Way)*, Nāgārjuna elaborates a theory that he calls the "Eight Negations of the Middle Way." At the beginning of *Mūlamadhyamakakārikā*, he provides a dedicatory verse:

> I prostrate to the Perfect Buddha,
> The best of teachers, who taught that
> Whatever is dependently arisen is
> Unceasing, unborn,
> Unannihilated, not permanent,
> Not coming, not going,
> Without distinction, without identity,
> And free from conceptual construction[1]

Here, Nāgārjuna offers a unique interpretation of the teachings of the Buddha, who advocated the "middle way," which does not adhere to one extreme or another, as the right path to follow.

One of the basic concepts in Buddhism is that of *pratītyasamutpāda* (dependent origination; Japanese *engi*), which refers to the belief that all things do not exist independently but rather in causal relationships with all events and circumstances, and sometimes in the interdependent relationships with contrasting or opposing things. Nāgārjuna's "Eight Negations of the Middle Way" are also linked to this concept. While neither theory is simple nor straightforward enough for a layman to explain, the act of refusing to accept absolute values, not adhering to one extreme or another, and being aware of the relationship between opposing existences is, at the very least, worth pondering at the present moment, when the world is divided by binary value judgments, and all manner of value systems are undergoing repeated shifts and transformations. The notion of the middle way is richly suggestive in post-pandemic societies in particular, where a kind of fluid equilibrium between human safety, health, and economic activity is being sought out.

The practice and the community of contemporary art are now supported by a global network that stretches to every corner of the world, but even in the art world, which has long been focused on the developments in the West, a number of values are shifting. Evaluations and historical reassessments of works by non-Western artists from diverse genders and races are also gaining momentum. While there is some kind of shared canon, other histories are being added that amplify and provide multiple layers. It is no longer possible to reach a true understanding of works produced in any period or region without deciphering the causal relationships and genealogies between them, as well as the unique historical, social, economic, and cultural contexts of each country or region. The same might also be said of Prabhavathi Meppayil's practice, which at first glance does not reveal the concrete symbols or information that might offer a representation of her background or environment. However, by deciphering the multilayered nature and fusion of the opposing qualities in her artworks, we can discern and enjoy the unique worldview inscribed within, that is unconstrained by simple categories. From the perspective of a globally shared canon of art history, Meppayil's recent practice is perhaps reminiscent of the work of Agnes Martin and others through its visual connection to Minimalism, especially in terms of its delicacy. While various arguments could be made about Martin's position in relation to Minimalism, it is useful in any case to have a shared reference point through which peripheral regions of the world have observed the development of Western-centric art. This reference also serves as a point of entry that allows us to decipher Meppayil's work.

Representations that share something in common with Minimalism and geometric abstraction, on the one hand, can also be seen in the often abstract and geometric diagrams of cosmological structures found in ancient Indian religious beliefs. For example, in Jainism, the structure of the universe is graphically represented as an elaborately quantified cosmic space; while cosmic maps with Mount Sumeru, the central axis of the universe in Buddhist cosmology, are often organized in a geometric manner and projected onto mandalas and other objects. The five elements of the universe are also visualized by stupas in various parts of the world, while the *gorinto* (the five-ringed Buddhist pagoda) that developed in Japan is stacked upwards in order of the elements of earth, water, fire, wind, and sky, which correspond in turn to the cubic, spherical, pyramidal, hemispherical, and jewel-shaped forms respectively. The cosmic egg from which the Hindu creator god Brahma was born is an extremely minimal representation of the universe. Tantric paintings from Rajasthan and other parts of India also contain minimalistic representations of cosmic spheres, pyramids, arrows, and spirals somewhat reminiscent of the work of Kazimir Malevich. Tantric paintings contain symbolism in the form of colors and shapes and are created for meditative purposes. As a rule, their creators are anonymous, and similarly abstracted worldviews have long run parallel to the Indian tradition of highly decorative and colorful religious paintings and detailed miniatures. Against the backdrop of this cultural history, Western art techniques were introduced to India through the arts and crafts schools established by the British during the late nineteenth century, while the history of modernism also permeated the country during the early twentieth century.

With this multilayered cultural background in mind, I would like to advance several possible polyvalent interpretations of Meppayil's abstract works. Both her flat copper-wire series and the metalworking series that uses the tool called a *thinnam* move between two- and three-dimensional frameworks and often embrace characteristics of painting and sculpture. The copper-wire pieces are created by applying more than ten layers of gesso, scratching the surface in order to embed the copper wire as if to make a drawing, applying another ten or more layers of gesso, and finally scraping out the surface. When displayed on the wall, these works could be considered two-dimensional, but in reality they are massive three-dimensional works. When displayed horizontally on the floor, these pieces seem to resemble minerals carved out of geological formations. The thinnam works are accumulations of small tool marks and are displayed in a flat manner, more like semi-solid reliefs. As mentioned earlier, considering their minimalistic visual elements, some of the copper-wire works appear almost completely white from a distance; even the thinnam series is difficult to recognize when viewed from far away. It is also extremely difficult for the camera lens to capture these works from a single perspective, and only when a viewer actually concentrates on the details and shifts their perspective across the surface do the finish and the material aspects of the work begin to eloquently speak.

Meppayil grew up in a family of goldsmiths, and she has been familiar with the thinnam tool since her childhood. I visited her studio and the goldsmith store run by her family in Bangalore around ten years ago, and the shopping street where they were located was bustling with activity and full of traditional artisans, including metalworkers. Bangalore, the country's third largest city, is now the center of the IT industry and known as India's Silicon Valley; therefore, its traditional industries must surely have been greatly affected by the emergence of the IT industry, with the role of handicraft gradually dwindling. The ornamental tools used in the metalworking trade certainly hold more meaning for Meppayil than just found objects—memories of many unknown craftsmen are contained within each small metal cube. By weaving a few organic shapes into the geometric forms, Meppayil avoids the extreme perfection and elimination of traces of handiwork—goals of Minimalism. Hundreds of small metal cubes of different types (iron, copper, and brass) are arranged on the wall, based on a meticulous plan, so that the overall image can be seen as a mandala, projecting an image of the entire universe.

Metal, used in both series, is one of the most common material families found in modernist sculpture. Cold and imposing, metal is used in monuments to project power and authority, but Meppayil uses only a small amount of metal to avoid the impression of heaviness or mass. She uses copper wire, as if she were making a drawing with pencil lines; and she makes marks with the thinnam tool on the gesso surface, as if she were drawing dots with a flat brush. Meppayil has an exhaustive understanding of metal as a material, and she carries out a dialogue with it, finding herself drawn to the shape and form that it demands of her even as she leverages its natural properties during her creative process. This working

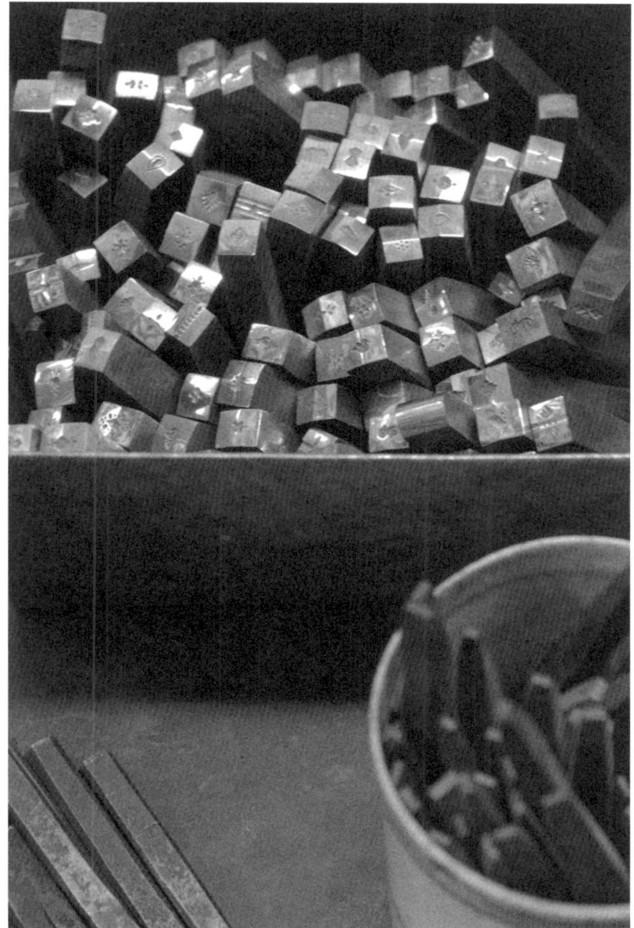

Thinnam tools

process, which is likely related to the temperature and humidity at the time of creation, involves control, as channeled through the will of the artist, and a relinquishing of that same control by letting nature take its course. While most Minimalist artists in America focus on the concept and the finished form, with the production itself often outsourced to factories, Meppayil's works are created through her own handiwork as a craftsperson, as she needs to listen to the "voice of the material." Here, there is no separation between the concept and the actual production: rather, there is an ambivalence between the notion of the artist and the artisan. Also, the heat from the artist's palm is conducted through the copper wire and the thinnam during production, transforming the metal from a symbol of coldness to an object imbued with human body heat and the memory of the hand. It is a warm Minimalism, so to speak. This process also calls to mind the temperature and humidity of Bangalore's climate, while the gesso underlay reminds us of the texture of plaster walls, which are moist and cool in the shade even on a very warm day. In this sense, we can also feel the warmth of Martin's body in her paintings, where she used rulers and masking tape but also drew lines in pencil, leaving behind traces of the artist's hand.

Martin talks about a certain meditative element in the process of making her work, which equally induces a state of meditation in the viewer. The long periods of time that Meppayil spends applying repeated layers of gesso before scraping them off again can also be a kind of meditative labor. The work she creates encompasses all of the time, spaces, and universes in which she has lived within its minimal visual elements. Here, cultures both Western and Eastern, languages, religions, the histories of various peoples, and her own personal history and memories, including those of her own family, are projected. Meditation is the act of sublimating one's consciousness to a higher and loftier dimension, removed from immediate reality. Standing in front of Prabhavathi Meppayil's works and listening to their voice in that moment, even as we find ourselves in a world where everything is in constant flux, perhaps we will be able to relish an encounter with her in some different dimension.

Mami Kataoka is Chief Curator at Mori Art Museum
Translated from the Japanese by Darryl Jingwen Wee

1 *The Fundamental Wisdom of the Middle Way: Nāgārjuna's Mūlamadhyamakakārikā*, translation and commentary by Jay L. Garfield (New York: Oxford University Press, 1995), 2.

Being with the work and in the work
An Interview with Prabhavathi Meppayil

Wells Fray-Smith I want to start with your beginnings as an artist—you studied painting at the Ken School of Art in Bangalore, India, during the early 1990s. The school had a reputation for being open, democratic, and embracing modernism. Can you speak a bit about your education and what affect it had on you?

Prabhavathi Meppayil My association with Ken School of Art began when I was ten years old and I tagged along with my sister, who was a hobby student there. I was fascinated by the ambience of the school and the teacher Rudrappa Mallappa Hadapad's drawing and painting demonstrations, especially the portraits. This bewilderment stayed with me, and Hadapad was an uncompromising artist with an experimental approach to art that challenged a lot of accepted notions. This shaped my understanding of a certain way of approaching modernism. He used to tell his students that "art elevates you, encountering an artwork transforms you as a person," and this influenced my understanding of art and its significance in life. It also holds true personally at a moment when the world is in a dark place due to the pandemic. When you are questioning the very significance of life, perhaps art helps in the healing process.

Wells Fray-Smith Your work has a graphic quality with a strong emphasis on line, detailed mark-making, and the use of the *thinnam*, but your early work was figurative—you drew figures and animals on gesso. In 2010, you began working on abstract, wall-mounted panels embedded with copper wire or small indentations. What prompted this shift from figuration to abstraction?

Prabhavathi Meppayil I began experimenting and exploring possibilities with materials in the late 1990s. During this time, I came across traditional wall-painting techniques and gesso panels. Wall painting is one of the earliest mediums of painting, and it's very disciplined and process oriented. It has a long history in the Indian art context; for example, the extraordinary fresco paintings of the Ajanta Caves (c. 1st century BCE–6th century CE) located in the north-central Maharashtra state and the Sittanavasal Cave (2nd century BCE) in the southeast Tamil Nadu state. I was intrigued by the process of making the gesso panel and the technique of painting or drawing on the panel as a way to revisit the history of painting.

My figurative paintings were subjective and punctuated with mark-making using thinnam tools, the tool used by goldsmiths to make delicate patterns on bangles. The object-like quality of the panel inspired me to push the boundaries further—to explore how a finely made gesso panel, with its subdued glossy-white surface, was more than just a surface for painting, but an object in itself. From then, I emphasized the physical aspect of the gesso panel, the process, and the materials to explore the conceptual concerns of the art language and the everyday.

Wells Fray-Smith You experiment with two types of panel: one with copper wire embedded in the gesso and the other with subtle indentations made by a thinnam tool. The panels often follow the logic of the grid and seem meticulously planned. What role does chance play in your process of making a panel?

Prabhavathi Meppayil There is always a chance factor in my work. The construction of lines in the copper-wire panel may look similar to another panel, but they are always different. And in the thinnam panels, each mark depends on the tap of the tool to make the indentation in the gesso. The process of preparing the panel is disciplined, but the outcome is dependent on the material and process—from applying the gesso layers to how the wires are stretched and the intensity of the sanding process. I think of sanding as blind painting because my face is covered with so much protective gear; so much so that I cannot completely control what comes through. In their own way, the copper wires unravel through the layers of sanded gesso; I cannot control it. Materials have a life of their own, and the element of serendipity makes the materials compelling to engage with.

Wells Fray-Smith Could you describe the process of making a panel from start to finish?

untitled-cu3-2011, 2011 (detail)

Prabhavathi Meppayil It is a labor-intensive process that starts with a wooden panel. Like painting, the unbleached cloth is stretched over the wooden panel and then coated with gesso by hand. Layers and layers of thin gesso are applied, which makes the panel strong. For the copper-wire works, I apply twenty coats and then embed the wire, and then I add another ten to fifteen coats. The thinnam panel needs more layers, at least thirty. I always make a couple of panels at a time, in part because of the quantity of the gesso needed for each. With Bangalore weather, I can maybe do two or three coats of gesso per day.

After about six days of layering, when the base is really dry, I start to embed the copper wire. Stretching the wire is very, very tricky. The material has a life of its own, and I have to listen to it. I repeat the process of layering gesso until the copper wire is concealed, and once the gesso has dried, I sand the surface with a sanding machine and then finally by hand.

For the thinnam panel, I start on a sanded panel and work horizontally. Initially when I started the thinnam work, I was guided by the sound. It really makes a noise as you hit the tool. I saw the marks as the absence of sound—the remnants after you have used the tool, removed it, and the sound is gone. I remember my father, who was a goldsmith, tapping the tool on gold bangles. ... There is a certain rhythm to it. Most of my work is completely dictated by material and medium. The whole process of making the panel is performative but also meditative because of the total involvement, the kind of attention, the kind of focus in the work. It is the process of being with the work and in the work.

Wells Fray-Smith So, you can read the thinnam panel like a score—each mark is a visual residue of the sound?

Prabhavathi Meppayil Yes, and as children we were fascinated by the sound of the tools tapping, and my father would let us try them. For me, the indents on the panel are evocative of this rhythm, and they are a loss, a collection of loss. I listen to the sounds of everyday life. Where I live, in the goldsmith's hub in the old part of Bangalore, you keep hearing the tapping sound of gold and other metals. Even now, can you hear that? [A consistent tapping sound in different pitches can be heard.] There is a sort of rhythm in it, isn't there? To quote the American composer John Cage, "Wherever we are, what we hear is mostly noise. When we ignore it, it disturbs us. When we listen to it, we find it fascinating."

Wells Fray-Smith When you are making the panel, do you plan the composition and arrangement of the marks in advance? Or is it a rhythm that you follow to decide the position of the next mark?

Prabhavathi Meppayil The thinnam tool is traditionally meant to be used vertically from top to bottom, but on the panel, I started making marks horizontally, either from left to right or vice versa, almost like a script. I follow the rhythm, and there is a certain guideline as I move horizontally with the tap. Placing the marks one next to the other needs focus. You have to be in it, in the moment of making. Thinnam work has a rhythm of time inherent in its making.

Wells Fray-Smith It seems that the human being is so embedded in your work. Your work is often discussed in relation to Minimalism or the aesthetics of the grid, but I'm interested in the human as a trope—how the body is present in the work but never pictorialized, and how the body animates the architectural spaces of your installations.

Prabhavathi Meppayil The human aspect is not apparent or consciously visible in my work, and I have not spoken about it much. My work is often read as being about the artist, the practice, and the craft because I come from a family of goldsmiths and because that history is there, but it's not as simple as that. I am critically engaging with the language of the work through the context of my lived experience. This is where the histories of artisanal practice, or personal narratives, come into the picture and overlap with the visible geometric vocabulary. In the grid installations *sb/eighteen* (2018) (pp. 42–43) and *tw/one* (2016) (pp. 106–107), for example, the grid is made from found objects (molds), and most of the molds were from my father's collection. They had been used for many years in the artisanal process, and now obsolete, they are devoid of their original purpose. When the molds are reiterated as art objects, it is difficult to solely read them as Minimalist, simple forms because they come with individual histories that I want to engage with. Unlike the industrial objects of the 1970s, these molds are handmade and used by individuals; there is a human touch. The socio-cultural history and context of the objects add layers to the complexity of the language.

In the installation *Melting Pot* (2009) that I did in Bangalore, I made marks with the thinnam tool on rubble that I had collected around my place. I situated this pile of rubble in the interior of a modern building. It was a comment on the movement of people from one place to the other, and migration and the changing landscape of the city.

Wells Fray-Smith I am struck by your numerical titles of *tw/one* and *sb/eighteen*. Can you say more about how you title your work?

Prabhavathi Meppayil I did not want the titles of my works to be representational or to preempt interpretations, and therefore, I came up with a naming system. Each work is named by a number (in letters) affixed to an abbreviated version of the show's name or the place or the year. Works for an exhibition in London were titled as *l/ninety five*, and the Berlin show works as *BerlinSeptember/Six*, and so on. Sometimes the titles are markers of time and markers of a process; the concrete sculpture titling (for example, *eighteen one zero-0525*, 2019) (p. 36) is the volume of the geometric form and the time of casting the concrete mold.

Wells Fray-Smith Since the last book *nine seventeen* in 2014, your work has developed quite considerably. You're still making panels, but they have begun to take on new shapes, with new forms and in new repetitions, and you have moved into an increasingly sculptural and architectural direction, using three dimensions as the stage to encounter your work, as in *Melting Pot*. How do you define yourself and your work—as a painter, a sculptor, an installation artist—and why?

Prabhavathi Meppayil This is difficult to answer. I started off as a painter, but then I moved on. Basically, I enjoy the process of making. But I think my engagement with space started much before 2014. One of the site-specific installations, *rw/seventeen* (pp. 124–125), which I did at Galleryske in Bangalore in 2013, was a reflected version of the ceiling. I stretched copper wire on the wall with the slanted parallel lines following the lines on the roof. It was about the coming together of two different spaces: the imaginary space, subtly hinted at by the drawing of the lines/wires, and the actual architectural space.

The work titled *dp/sixteen/part one* (2015–16) (p. 103) for the Dhaka Art Summit in 2016 continued the main idea of creating movement between floor and ceiling, the outside and inside. The coffered ceiling in the site seemed as

untitled series-3, 2010 (detail)

though it could be a series of empty cubes arranged in a grid on the ceiling. I thought it would be interesting to recreate the coffered ceiling on the floor, to create tension/movement between the floor and ceiling. In some ways the idea was to virtually bring the floor and ceiling to float on the same plane. I recreated the ceiling by making a grid of cubes on the floor. Needless to say, this work was located in the city where one of the most significant architectural buildings of our time, the National Assembly Hall by Louis Kahn, existed.

Wells Fray-Smith This conversation has highlighted that your work destabilizes fixed categories; for example, it's not just two dimensional or three dimensional. I see that position—of categories being fluid—visibly in the work, as well. There's an experience of perceiving emptiness in the panels before getting close and realizing they are full of marks; you have a meticulous process, but you welcome chance; there is repetition between panels but also difference; and conceptually, they move between modernism and Minimalism with strong human narratives. It's very difficult to categorize what you do and how the work operates.

Prabhavathi Meppayil I think the ambiguity of the gesso panel itself and the lack of clarity on its position is interesting. It is neither a painting nor an object. Same with the installation *sb/eighteen* or the concrete cubes. It is neither this nor that. I think the ambiguity or neutrality opens up the possibilities and also multiplies its readings. For instance, the installation *se/one half* (2017–18) (pp. 76–77), where a series of copper wire panels were placed on plinths horizontally, appears to be floating on the floor beneath the skylight. The panels trace the changing light of the day, with shadow patterns falling on the work. Here, the gesso panel is viewed in a different orientation, which subtly subverts the way you perceive the work.

Scale also plays an important role in the panels and how they are perceived. I find different scales have different resonances with viewers, different contributions to the visual experience. When you're in front of a small panel you might have a particular visual sensation because of what is in your visual field; you have an intimate experience of the work, and you can view the line from edge to edge. Whereas in the large panels, like the untitled-cu1 series (2011–12) or *n/ninety two* (2016) (p. 101), the experience is very different. The lines play hide and seek, coming in and out of vision. I think it is very interesting to show the smaller and larger work together for this reason. I like the performative aspect to viewing.

Wells Fray-Smith What about the shaped panels you have been making? They use the logic of the grid, but suddenly break with its form. You've added curved sides, quite literally bending modernism's rules of linearity. What led you to shaped canvases?

Prabhavathi Meppayil Instead of arbitrarily deciding the shape of the panels, I let the tool determine the shape; the panel is the shape of the thinnam tool. It was interesting to notice that the geometric form in thinnam tools is not a pure form, as you see in the narrative of abstraction. It is slippery. In a single thinnam tool, you can find multiple geometric forms. The shaped panels are a reflection of the same. *l/hundred fifty eight* (2019) (p. 52) and *forty five nineteen* (2019) (p. 73) are enlarged versions of the multiple geometric forms in the thinnam tool. These forms or patterns have been around for many years, as I said earlier. With its individual cultural history, it is difficult to fit these into a linear narrative of modernism.

Wells Fray-Smith is Assistant Curator: Special Projects at Whitechapel Gallery
This interview took place on October 9, 2020, with follow-up conversations in early 2021

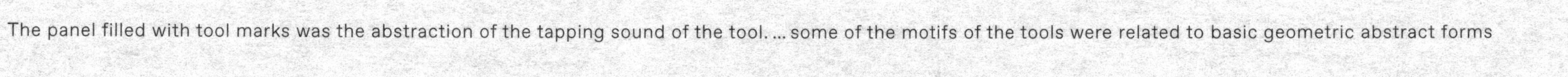
The panel filled with tool marks was the abstraction of the tapping sound of the tool. ... some of the motifs of the tools were related to basic geometric abstract forms

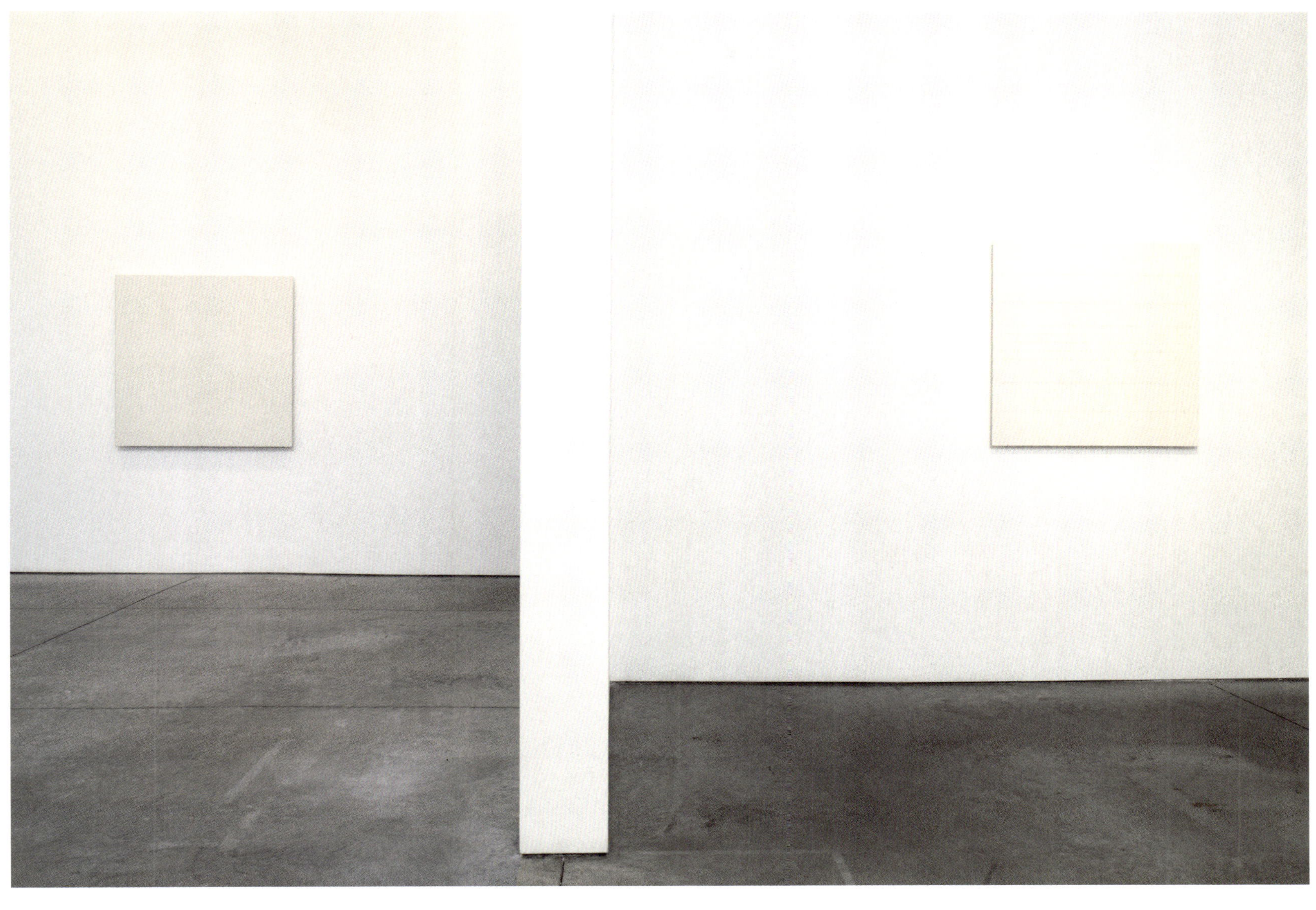

installation view Pace Gallery, New York, 2016

installation view   Pace Gallery, New York, 2016

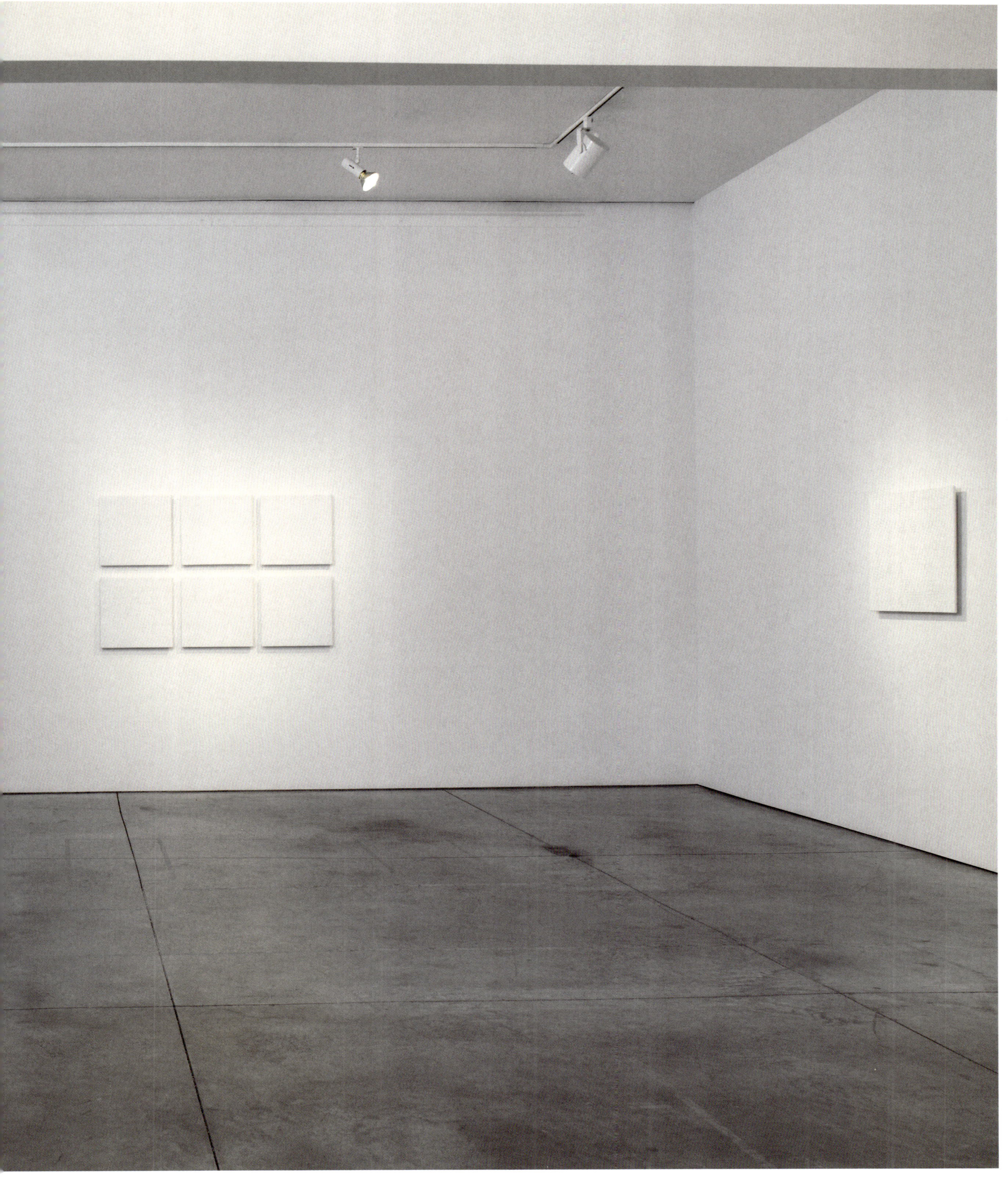

installation views Pace Gallery, New York, 2016

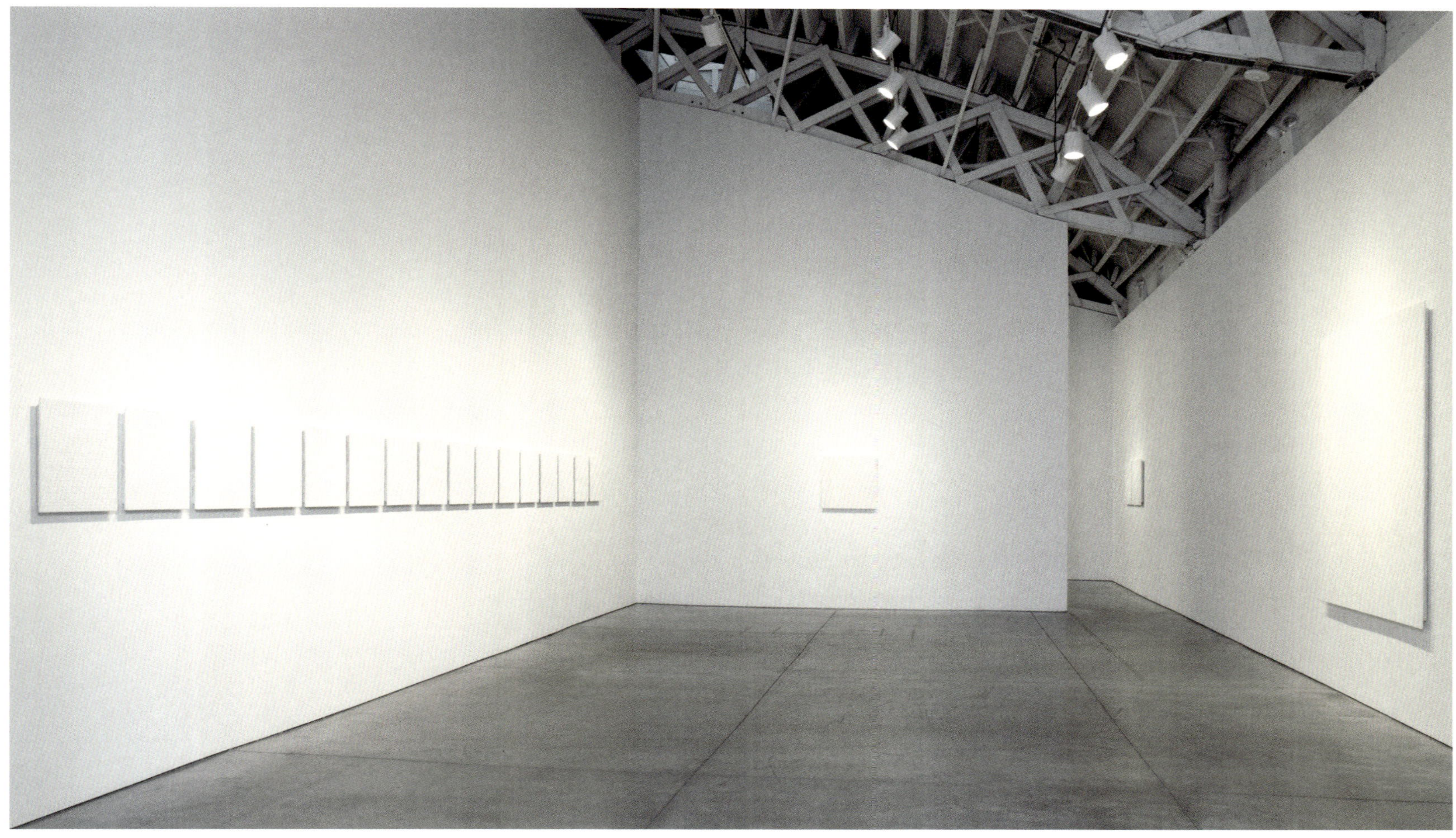

installation view   Dhaka Art Summit, 2016   dp/sixteen/part one, 2015–16   copper wire embedded in gesso cubes   (detail)

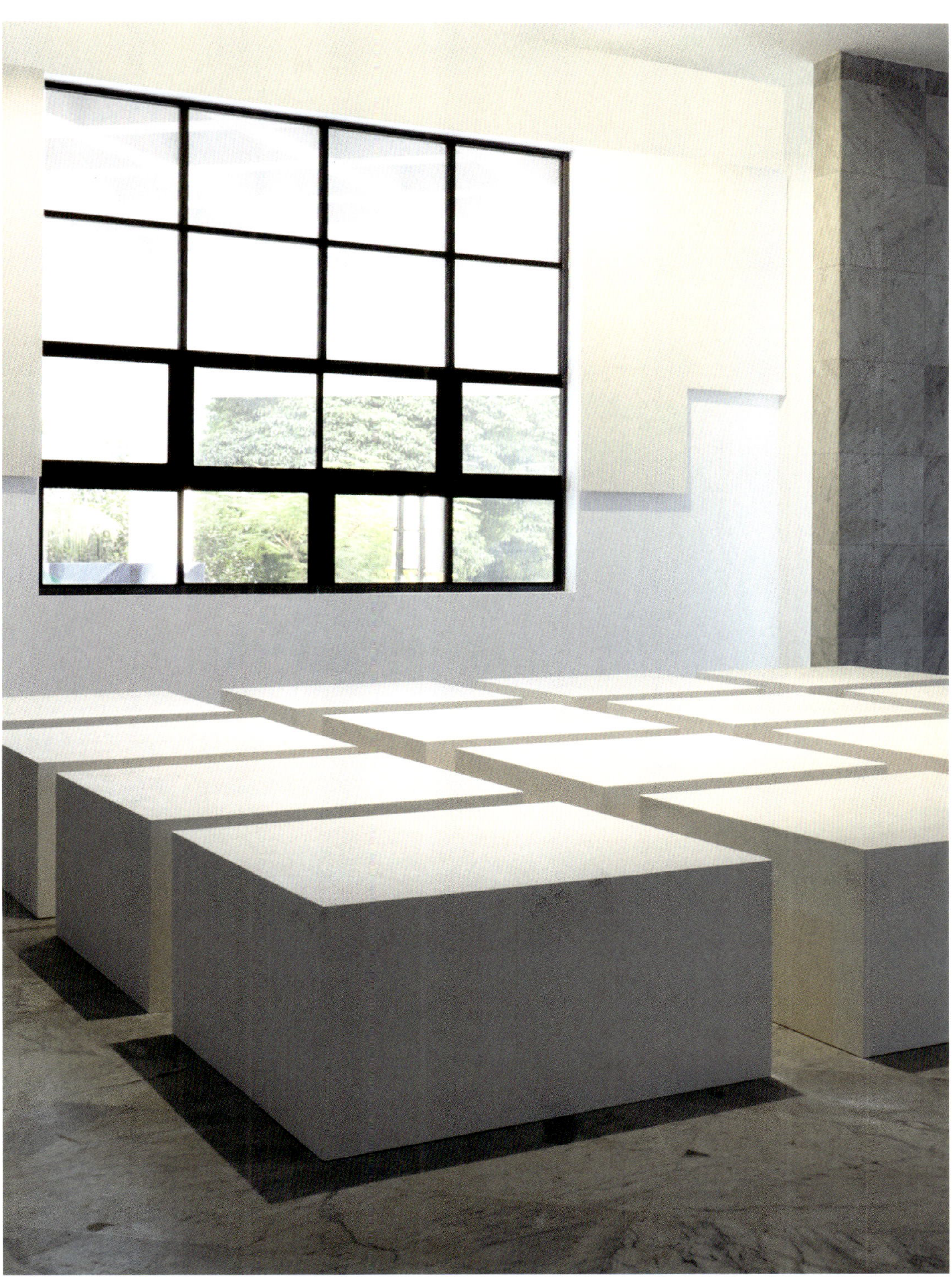

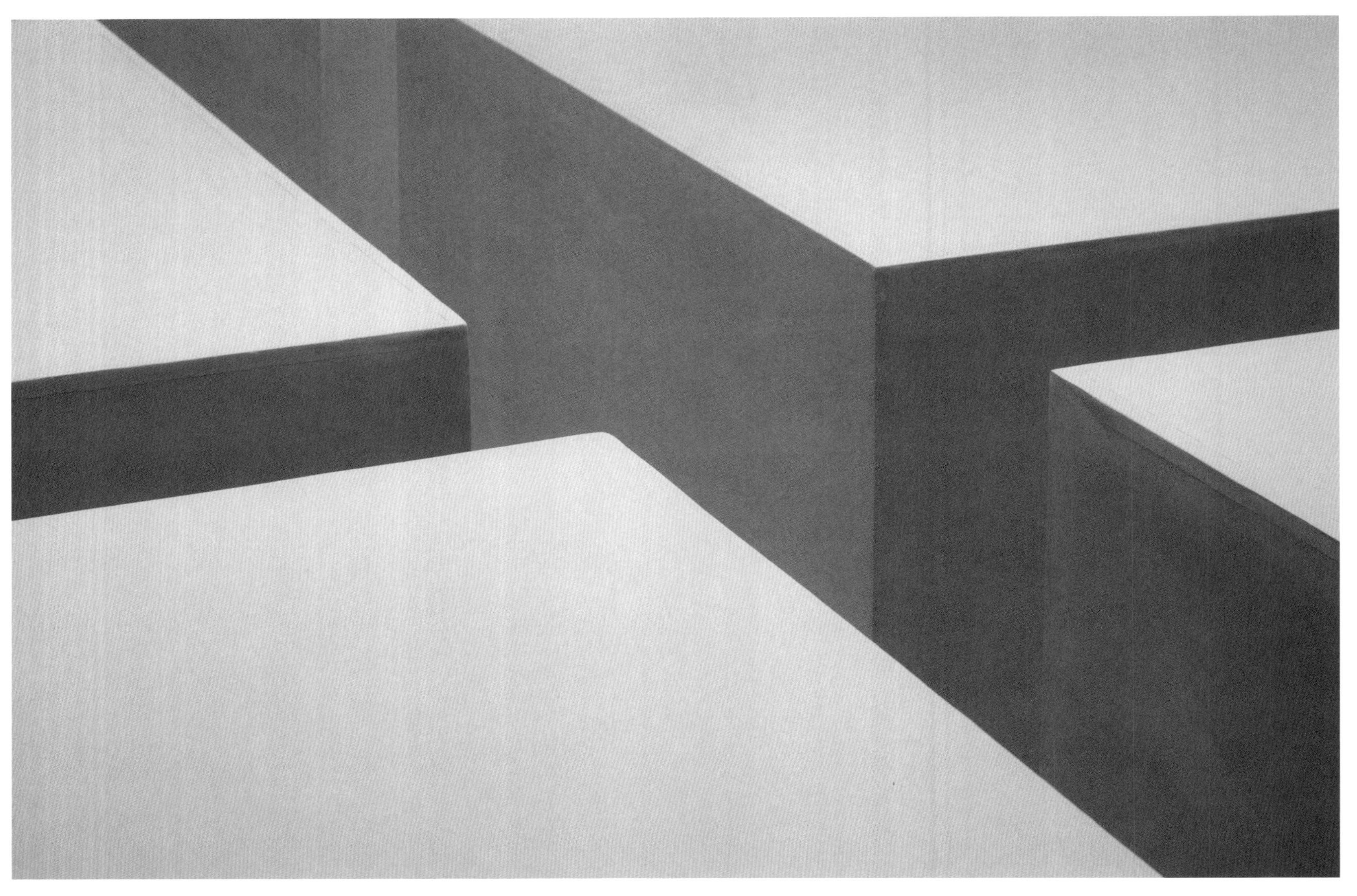

dp/sixteen/part one, 2015–16 (details)

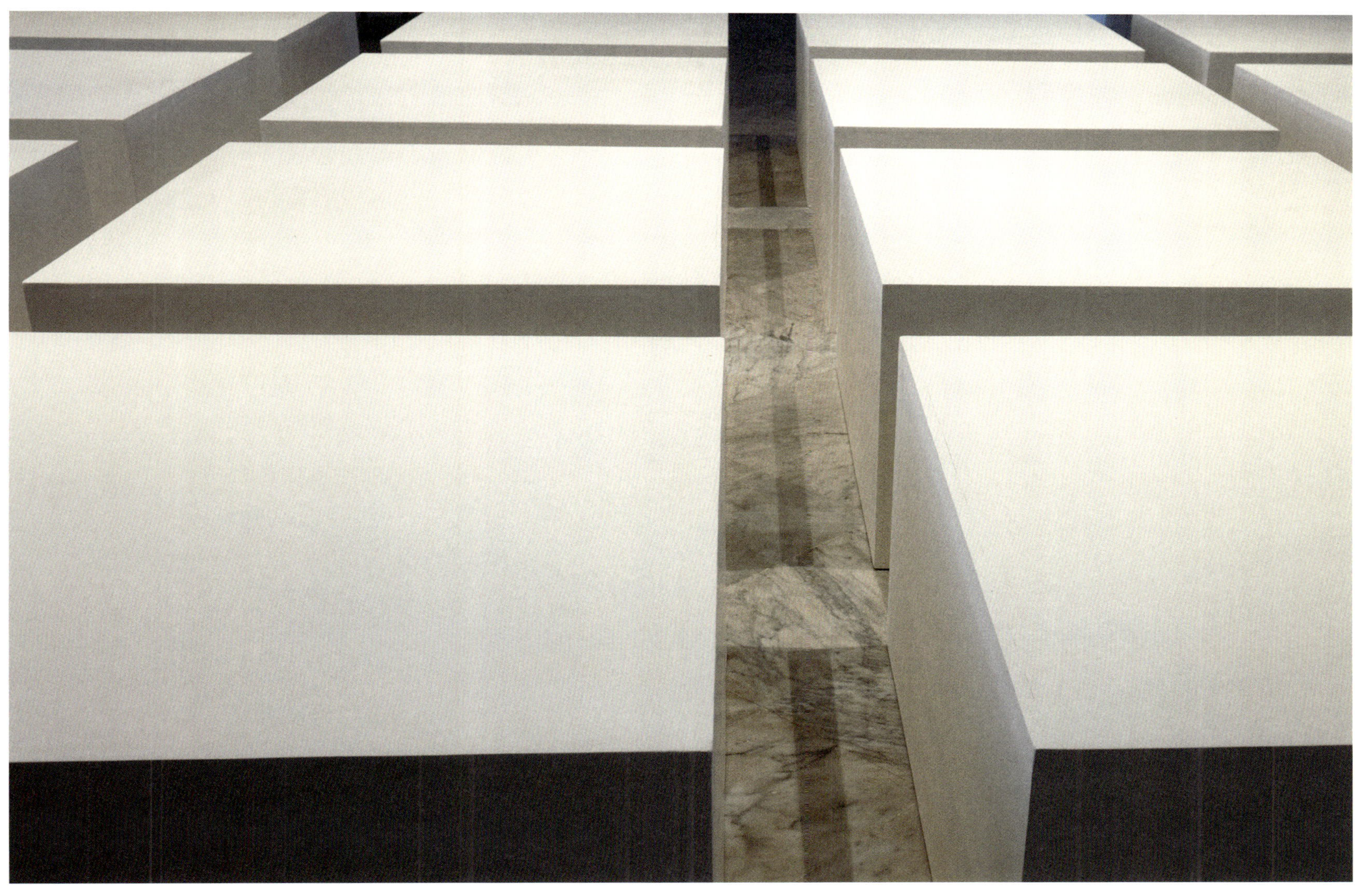

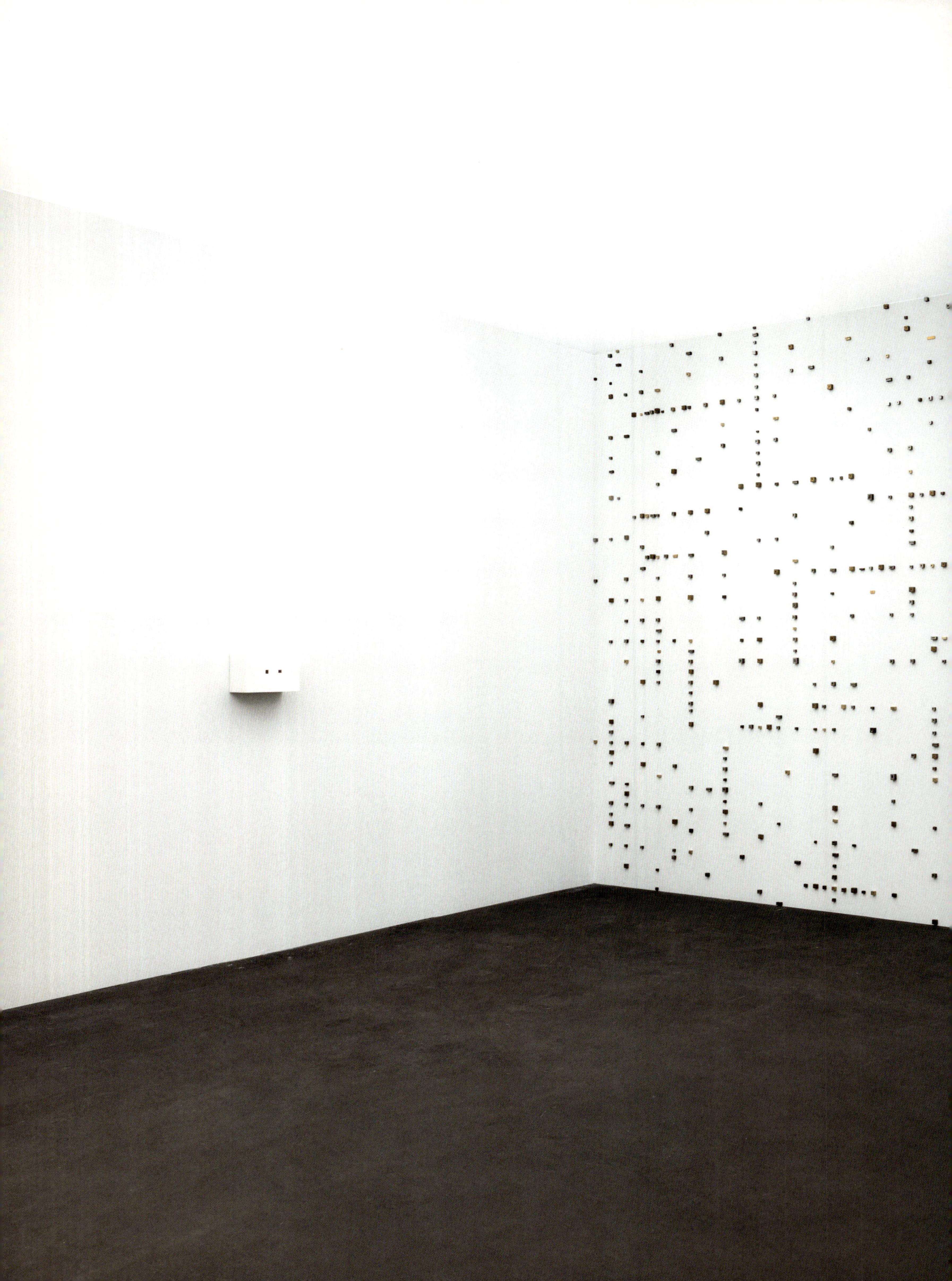

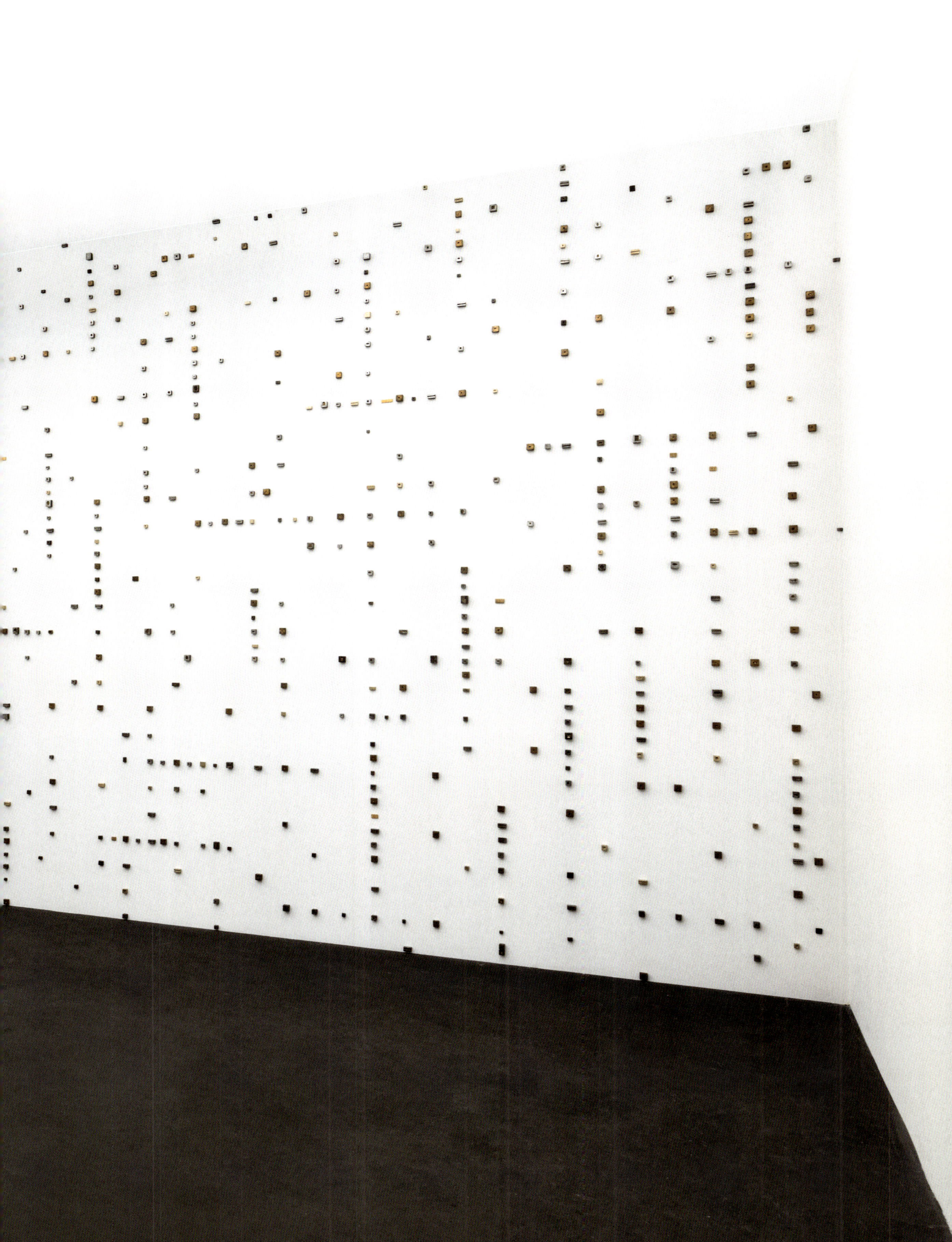

previous installation view Art Basel Unlimited, 2016 tw/one, 2016 found objects (iron and brass) and gesso cube above and opposite (details)

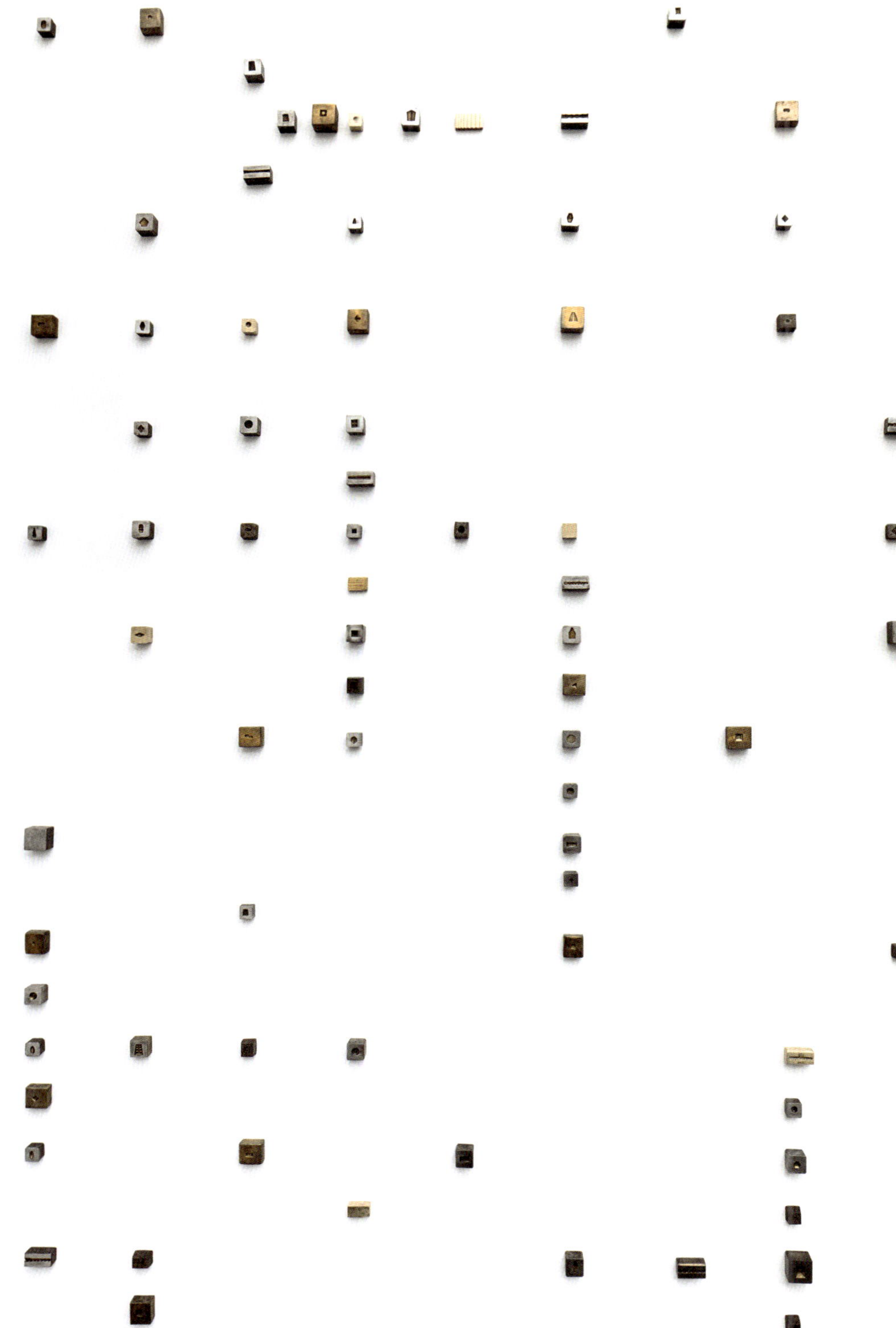

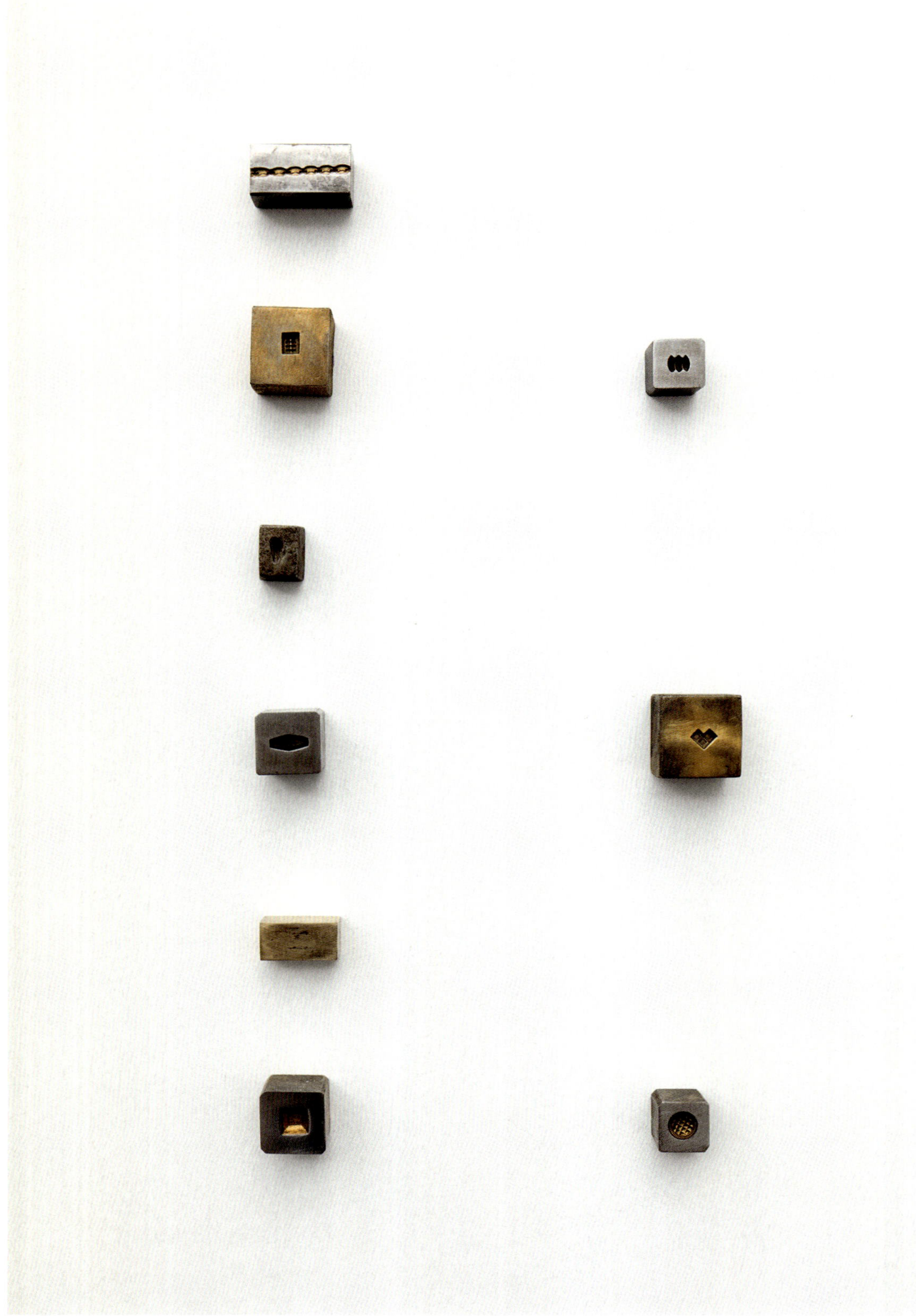

tw/one, 2016 (details)

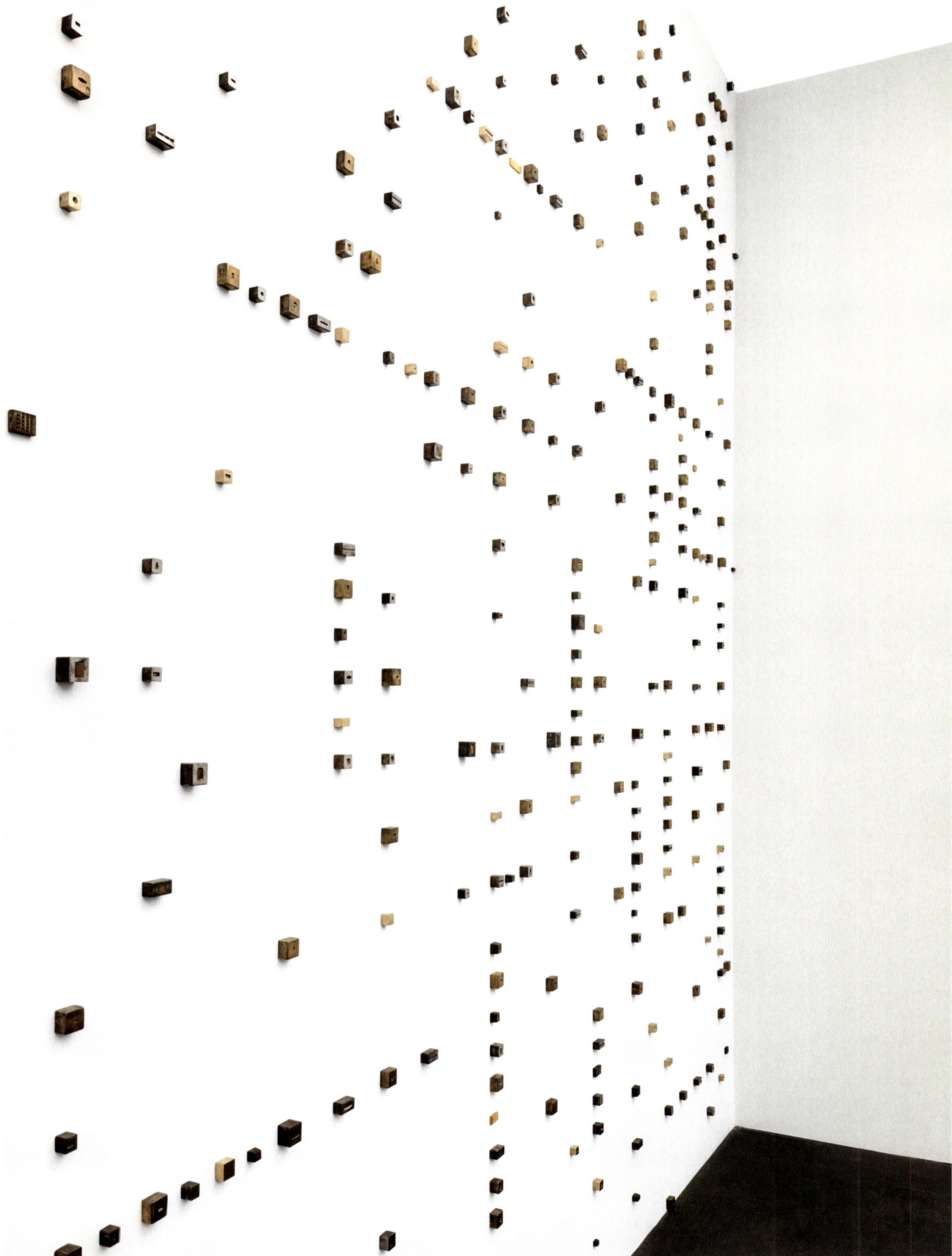

When I started working with the goldsmith’s tool, making indent marks on the panel, I began exploring the possibilities of mark-making

installation view American Academy in Rome, 2014 c2, 2014 copper wire embedded in gesso panel

previous installation view American Academy in Rome, 2014 opposite untitled series-3, 2010 thinnam on gesso panel (detail)

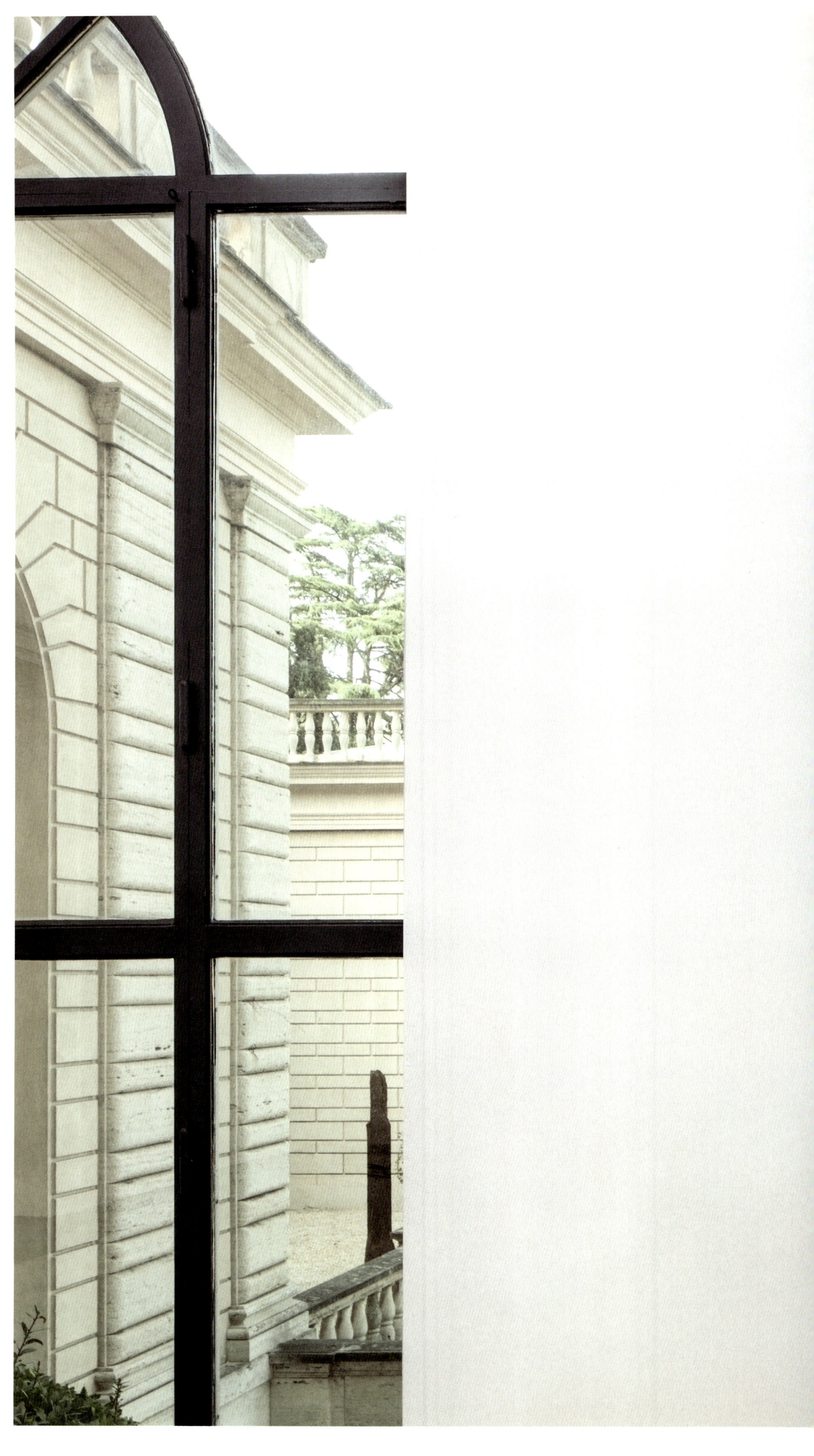

installation view American Academy in Rome, 2014 c5, 2013 copper wire embedded in gesso panel

c5, 2013 (detail)

untitled series-1, 2010 copper wire embedded in gesso panel (detail)

installation view Galleryske, Bangalore, 2013 rw/seventeen, 2013 copper wire site-specific installation

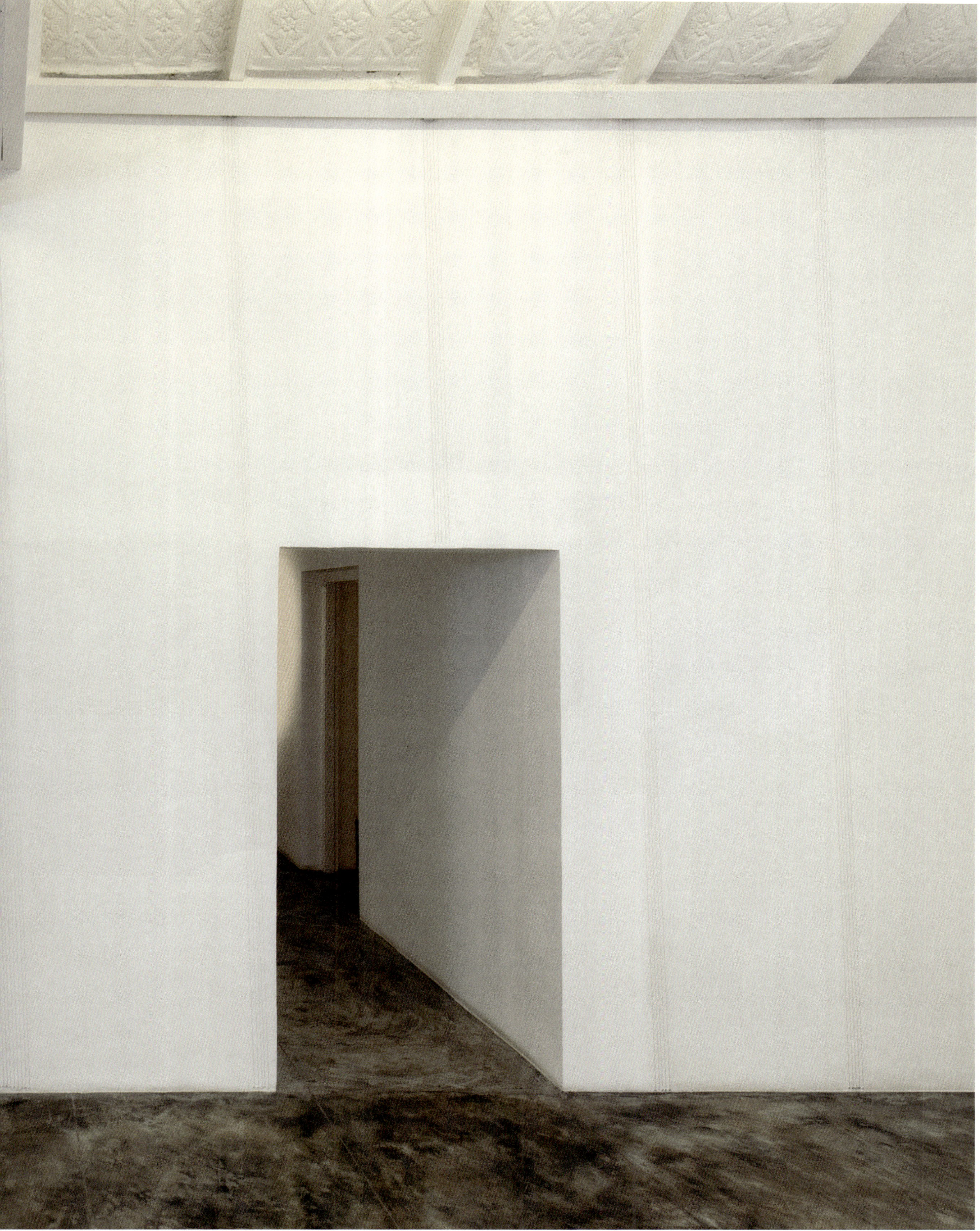

untitled-cu1-2011, 2011 copper wire embedded in gesso panel

untitled-cu1-2011, 2011 (detail)

installation view Venice Biennale, 2013

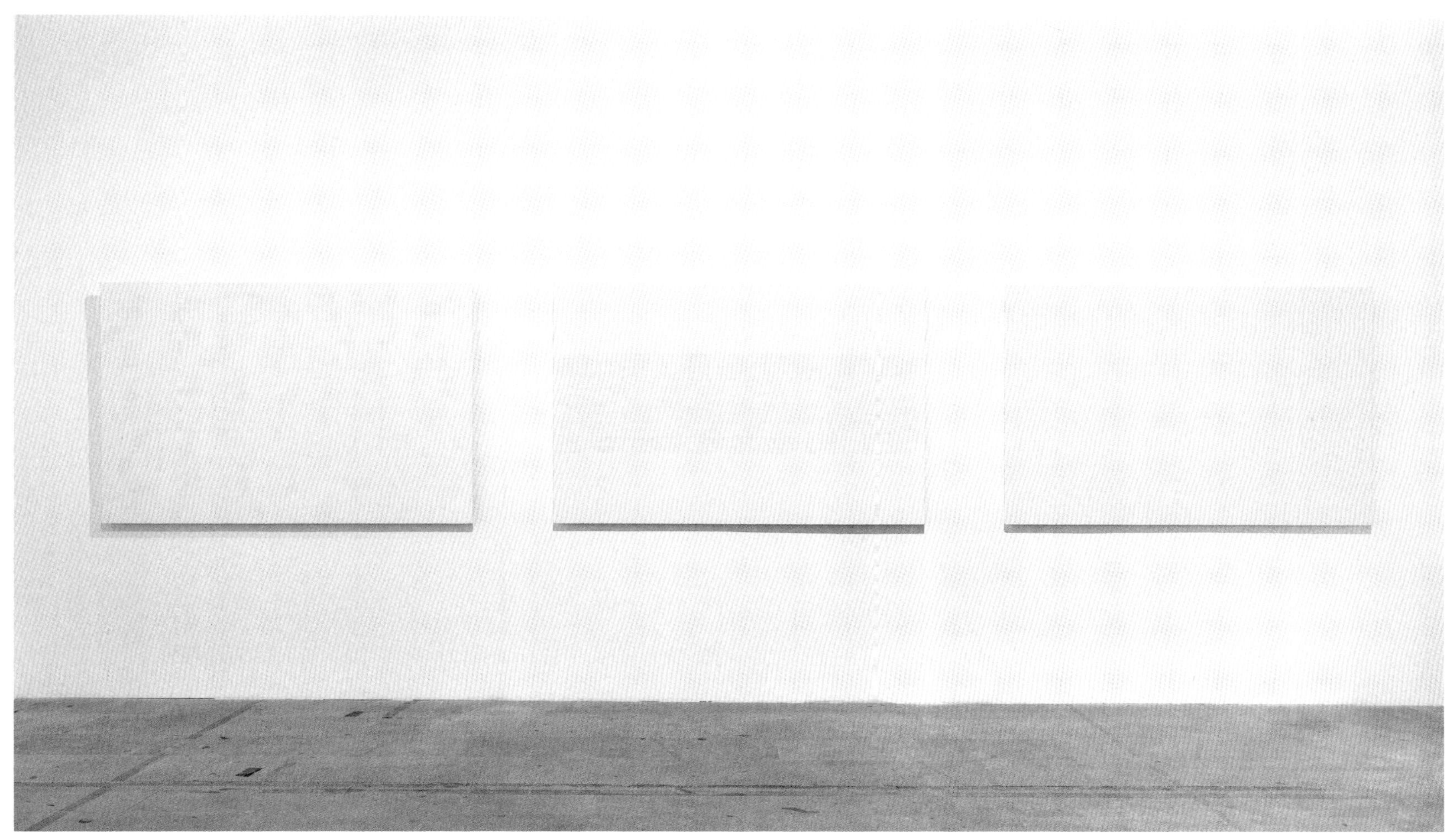

untitled-cu3-2011, 2011 copper wire embedded in gesso panel opposite (detail)

untitled-cu3-2011, 2011 (detail)

List of Works

17
fifty two twenty one, 2020
copper wire embedded in gesso panel
48 ⅛ × 48 ⅛ × 1 9⁄16" (122.2 × 122.2 × 4 cm)

18–19
fifty two twenty one, 2020 (details)

21
fifty one twenty one, 2020
copper wire embedded in gesso panel
48 ⅛ × 48 ⅛ × 1 9⁄16" (122.2 × 122.2 × 4 cm)

22
fifty one twenty one, 2020 (detail)

25
l/forty four, 2019
thinnam on gesso panels
16 panels, each 12 × 12 × 1 15⁄16"
(30.5 × 30.5 × 5 cm)

26–27
l/forty four, 2019 (details)

29
l/forty seven, 2018
copper wire embedded in gesso panel
48 × 48 × 1 15⁄16" (121.9 × 121.9 × 5 cm)

30–31
l/forty seven, 2018 (detail)

32–33
l/hundred eighteen, 2018
copper wire embedded in gesso panel
48 × 60 × 1 15⁄16" (121.9 × 152.4 × 5 cm)

34
l/hundred fifty nine, 2019
thinnam on gesso panel
48 × 48 × 1 15⁄16" (121.9 × 121.9 × 5 cm)

35
l/hundred fifty nine, 2019 (detail)

36
eighteen one zero-0525, 2019
concrete and copper
11 13⁄16 × 11 13⁄16 × 11 13⁄16" (30 × 30 × 30 cm)

37
(top)
thirty two five-0645, 2019
concrete and copper
11 13⁄16 × 11 13⁄16 × 11 13⁄16" (30 × 30 × 30 cm)

(bottom)
fifteen six zero-0630, 2019
concrete and copper
5 ⅞ × 14 15⁄16 × 14 15⁄16" (15 × 38 × 38 cm)

38–39
installation view
Pace Gallery, London, 2019

(left to right)
l/hundred thirty six, 2018
copper wire embedded in gesso panel
48 × 60 × 1 15⁄16" (121.9 × 152.4 × 5 cm)

thirty two five-0645, 2019
concrete and copper
11 13⁄16 × 11 13⁄16 × 11 13⁄16" (30 × 30 × 30 cm)

l/hundred fifty eight, 2019
thinnam on gesso panels
8 panels, each 18 × 12 × 1 15⁄16"
(45.7 × 30.5 × 5 cm)

l/hundred thirty one, 2018
copper wire embedded in gesso panel
48 × 48 × 1 15⁄16" (121.9 × 121.9 × 5 cm)

l/hundred eighty nine, 2018
copper wire embedded in gesso panel
48 × 48 × 1 15⁄16" (121.9 × 121.9 × 5 cm)

l/forty four, 2019
thinnam on gesso panels
16 panels, each 12 × 12 × 1 15⁄16"
(30.5 × 30.5 × 5 cm)

eighteen one zero-0525, 2019
concrete and copper
11 13⁄16 × 11 13⁄16 × 11 13⁄16" (30 × 30 × 30 cm)

40
fifteen six zero-0630, 2019
concrete and copper
5 ⅞ × 14 15⁄16 × 14 15⁄16" (15 × 38 × 38 cm)

41
thirty two five-0645, 2019
concrete and copper
11 13⁄16 × 11 13⁄16 × 11 13⁄16" (30 × 30 × 30 cm)

42–43
installation view
Pace Gallery, London, 2019

sb/eighteen, 2018
found objects (iron, copper, and brass)
and gesso
dimensions variable

45
sb/eighteen, 2018 (detail)

46–47
sb/eighteen, 2018 (details)

49
l/hundred ninety four, 2018
copper wire embedded in gesso panel
48 × 60 × 1 15⁄16" (121.9 × 152.4 × 5 cm)

50–51
l/hundred ninety four, 2018 (detail)

52
l/hundred fifty eight, 2019
thinnam on gesso panels
8 panels, each 18 × 12 × 1 15⁄16"
(45.7 × 30.5 × 5 cm)

53
l/hundred fifty eight, 2019 (detail)

55
forty three nineteen, 2019
thinnam on gesso panel
35 13⁄16 × 35 13⁄16 × 1 15⁄16" (91 × 91 × 5 cm)

56
forty three nineteen, 2019 (detail)

58–59
l/hundred thirty seven, 2019
thinnam on gesso panels
24 × 36 × 1 15⁄16" (61 × 91.4 × 5 cm)

60
l/hundred thirty seven, 2019 (detail)

61
dp/twenty/thirteen, 2019 (detail)

62–63
installation view
Dhaka Art Summit, 2020

dp/twenty/thirteen, 2019
copper wire and copper wire embedded
in gesso panel
dimensions variable

65
dp/twenty/six, 2019
thinnam on gesso panel
24 × 30 × 1 15⁄16" (60.9 × 76.2 × 5 cm)

66–67
dp/twenty/six, 2019 (details)

69
dp/twenty/forty eight, 2019
wood, gesso, and copper
30 × 30 × 1 15⁄16" (76.2 × 76.2 × 5 cm)

70
dp/twenty/forty eight, 2019 (detail)

73
forty five nineteen, 2019
thinnam on gesso panels
6 panels, each 24 × 24 × 1 15⁄16"
(60.9 × 60.9 × 5 cm)

74
d sixty four, 2017
gesso on found objects
28 3⁄8 × 28 3⁄8 × 1 9⁄16" (72 × 72 × 4 cm)

75
d sixty four, 2017 (detail)

76–77
installation view
Esther Schipper, Berlin, 2018

se/one half, 2017–18
copper wire embedded in gesso panels
12 panels, each 48 × 60 × 1 15⁄16"
(121.9 × 152.4 × 5 cm)

79
se/one half, 2017–18 (detail)

80–81
yt/twenty five, 2017 (details)
found objects (iron, copper, and brass)
dimensions variable

83
installation view
Yokohama Triennale, 2017

yt/forty two, 2017
copper wire and hook screws
dimensions variable

84
installation view
Yokohama Triennale, 2017

yt/forty two, 2017
copper wire and hook screws
dimensions variable

86–87
installation view
Drawing Room, London, 2017

(left)
twenty five seventeen, 2017
thinnam on gesso panel
48 × 48 × 1 3/8" (121.9 × 121.9 × 3.5 cm)

(right)
twenty six seventeen, 2017
copper wire embedded in gesso panel
48 × 60 × 1 3/8" (121.9 × 152.4 × 3.5 cm)

88
twenty six seventeen, 2017
copper wire embedded in gesso panel
48 × 60 × 1 3/8" (121.9 × 152.4 × 3.5 cm)

97
installation view
Pace Gallery, New York, 2016

(left)
n/eighty four, 2016
thinnam on gesso panel
48 × 47 15/16 × 1 1/2" (121.9 × 121.8 × 3.8 cm)

(right)
eight/fifteen, 2015
gold wire embedded in gesso panel
36 × 36 × 1 1/2" (91.4 × 91.4 × 3.8 cm)

98–99
installation view
Pace Gallery, New York, 2016

(left to right)
n/ninety one, 2016
copper wire embedded in gesso panel
48 × 60" (121.9 × 152.4 cm)

n/eighty two, 2016
thinnam on gesso panels
6 panels, each 18 × 18 × 1 3/16"
(45.7 × 45.7 × 3 cm)

n/eighty seven, 2016
copper wire embedded in gesso panel
24 × 30" (60.9 × 76.2 cm)

100
installation view
Pace Gallery, New York, 2016

(left)
n/eighty two, 2016
thinnam on gesso panels
6 panels, each 18 × 18 × 1 3/16"
(45.7 × 45.7 × 3 cm)

(right)
n/eighty seven, 2016
copper wire embedded in gesso panel
24 × 30" (60.9 × 76.2 cm)

101
installation view
Pace Gallery, New York, 2016

(left to right)
n/ninety three, 2016
copper wire embedded in gesso panels
16 panels, each 18 × 18" (45.7 × 45.7 cm)

n/eighty five, 2016
thinnam on gesso panel
24 × 24" (60.9 × 60.9 cm)

n/eighty six, 2016
thinnam on gesso panels
left panel 24 × 24" (60.9 × 60.9 cm)
right panel 24 × 30" (60.9 × 76.2 cm)

n/ninety two, 2016
copper wire embedded in gesso panel
72 × 71 1/2" (182.9 × 181.9 cm)

103
installation view
Dhaka Art Summit, 2016

dp/sixteen/part one, 2015–16 (detail)
copper wire embedded in gesso cubes
16 cubes, each 42 1/8 × 42 1/8 × 21 1/4"
(107 × 107 × 54 cm)

104–105
dp/sixteen/part one, 2015–16 (details)

106–107
installation view
Art Basel Unlimited, 2016

tw/one, 2016
found objects (iron and brass)
and gesso cube
dimensions variable

108–109
tw/one, 2016 (details)

110–111
tw/one, 2016 (details)

113
installation view
American Academy in Rome, 2014

c2, 2014
copper wire embedded in gesso panel
48 × 48 × 1½" (121.9 × 121.9 × 3.8 cm)

114–115
installation view
American Academy in Rome, 2014

(left)
untitled series-1, 2010
copper wire embedded in gesso panels
9 panels, each 18 1⁄16 × 18 1⁄16 × 1 3⁄8"
(45.8 × 45.8 × 3.5 cm)

(right)
c4, 2013
copper wire embedded in gesso panel
48 × 60 × 1½" (121.9 × 152.4 × 3.8 cm)

117
untitled series-3, 2010 (detail)
thinnam on gesso panel
48 × 72 × 1½" (121.9 × 182.8 × 3.8 cm)

118–119
installation view
American Academy in Rome, 2014

c5, 2013
copper wire embedded in gesso panel
24 1⁄8 × 30 1⁄8 × 1 5⁄16" (61 × 76.2 × 3.8 cm)

120–121
c5, 2013 (detail)

123
untitled series-1, 2010 (detail)

124–125
installation view
Galleryske, Bangalore, 2013

rw/seventeen, 2013
copper wire site-specific installation
dimensions variable

127
untitled-cu1-2011, 2011
copper wire embedded in gesso panel
48 × 72" (121.9 × 182.9 cm)

128
untitled-cu1-2011, 2011 (detail)

131
installation view
Venice Biennale, 2013

(left to right)
untitled-cu1-2011, 2011
copper wire embedded in gesso panel
48 × 72" (121.9 × 182.9 cm)

untitled-cu3-2011, 2011
copper wire embedded in gesso panel
48 × 72" (121.9 × 182.9 cm)

untitled-cu2-2011, 2011
copper wire embedded in gesso panel
48 × 72" (121.9 × 182.9 cm)

132
untitled-cu3-2011, 2011
copper wire embedded in gesso panel
48 × 72" (121.9 × 182.9 cm)

133
untitled-cu3-2011, 2011 (detail)

135
untitled-cu3-2011, 2011 (detail)

Biography

Born in 1965
Lives and works in Bangalore, India

1992 Diploma in Fine Arts, Ken School of Art, Bangalore
1986 B.A. Bangalore University

Solo Exhibitions

2019 *Recent Works*, Pace Gallery, London
2018 *b/seven eighths*, Esther Schipper, Berlin
2017 Galleryske, Vasant Kunj, New Delhi
2016 Pace Gallery, New York
2014 *berlinoneseven*, Johnen Galerie, Berlin
nine seventeen, American Academy in Rome and Pace Gallery, London
2013 *Recent Works*, Galleryske, Bangalore
2010 *Recent Works*, Vadehra Art Gallery, New Delhi
2007 *Recent Works*, Sakshi Gallery, Mumbai
2001 Forum Schlossplatz, Aarau, Switzerland
1999 Chitra Art Gallery, Bangalore

Selected Group Exhibitions

2021 *Little Things: Parts I & II*, Pace Gallery, Geneva
Modern in Your Life, BassamFellows, Ridgefield, Connecticut
Carve, Curve, Cane, R & Company, New York
We Do Not Dream Alone: Asia Society Triennial Part II, Asia Society, New York
The Lines Fall Where They May, curated by Jason Wee, STPI, Singapore
Lines Tell Everything about the Universe, Mori Art Museum, Tokyo

2020 *Fault Lines*, curated by Amanda Sroka, Philadelphia Museum of Art
Crafting Geometry: Abstract Art from South and West Asia, Sotheby's, New York
Dhaka Art Summit: Seismic Movements, curated by Diana Campbell Betancourt and Sean Anderson, Bangladesh Shilpakala Academy, Dhaka
Scripting Time, Memory, Ecology, curated by Roobina Karode, Kiran Nadar Museum of Art, New Delhi

2019 *Home Is a Foreign Place: Recent Acquisitions in Context*, The Met Breuer, New York

2018 *Cosmopolis #1.5: Enlarged Intelligence*, curated by Kathryn Weir, organized by Mao Jihong Arts Foundation in collaboration with the Centre Pompidou, Dong Jiao Ji Yi, Chengdu, China
Superposition: Art of Equilibrium and Engagement, curated by Mami Kataoka, 21st Biennale of Sydney, Art Gallery of New South Wales

2017 *Everything We Do Is Music*, curated by Shanay Jhaveri, Drawing Room, London
Traveled to: Kunsthaus Centre D'art Pasquart, Biel/Bienne, Switzerland
Yokohama Triennale 2017: Islands, Constellations & Galapagos, curated by Akiko Miki, Yokohama Museum of Art
The Horizontal, Cheim & Read, New York
The Mulberry Forest Becoming Ocean, curated by Shi-ne Oh, Esther Schipper, Berlin

2016 Kochi-Muziris Biennale 2016, curated by Sudarshan Shetty, Kochi, India
Accrochage, curated by Caroline Bourgeois, Punta della Dogana, Venice
Dhaka Art Summit, curated by Diana Campbell Betancourt, Bangladesh Shilpakala Academy, Dhaka

2015 *Codes of Culture*, Galleryske, New Delhi
Approaching Abstraction, Jhaveri Contemporary, Mumbai

2014 *Carte Blanche*, Pace Chesa Büsin, Zuoz, Switzerland

2013 *abc—art berlin contemporary*, Johnen Galerie, Berlin
The Encyclopedic Palace, Massimiliano Gioni, 55th International Art Exhibition, Venice Biennale
Delhi Inaugural Show, Galleryske, New Delhi

2012 *Everything/Nothing*, Galleryske, Bangalore
Phantoms of Asia: Contemporary Awakens the Past, curated by Mami Kataoka and Allison Harding, Asian Art Museum, San Francisco

2011 *Equator #1: Shadow Lines: Indonesia Meets India*, Biennale Jogja XI 2011 [11th Yogyakarta Biennale], curated by Suman Gopinath and Alia Swastika, Jogja National Museum, Yogyakarta, Indonesia

2010 *Orientations: Trajectories in Indian Art*, curated by Deepak Ananth, Foundation De 11 Lijnen, Oudenburg, Belgium

2008 *Chalo! India: A New Era of Indian Art*, curated by Akiko Miki, organized by Mori Art Museum, Tokyo. Traveled to: National Museum of Contemporary Art, Seoul; Essl Museum, Vienna
The Sakshi Show, Durbar Hall Art Gallery, Kochi

2007 *Horn Please, Narratives in Contemporary Indian Art*, curated by Bernard Fibicher and Suman Gopinath, Kunstmuseum Bern, Switzerland
Inaugural Show: New Space: Colaba, Sakshi Gallery, Mumbai
Soft Spoken, curated by Bose Krishnamachari, Bombay Art Gallery, Mumbai

2005 *The Inverted Tree*, curated by Marta Jakimowicz, Gallery Threshold, New Delhi
Double-Enders, organized by Jehangir Art Gallery and The Museum Gallery, Mumbai. Traveled to: Vadehra Art Gallery, New Delhi; Gallery Sumukha, Bangalore; Durbar Hall Art Gallery, Kochi
Span, Sakshi Gallery, Mumbai
Ten Years Ten Artists, Gästeatelier Krone Aarau 1995–2005, Aarau, Switzerland
South Asian Women Artists Residency Show, organised by Theertha, Finomenal Space Gallery, Colombo, Sri Lanka
Are We Like This Only?, curated by Vidya Shivadas, Vadehra Art Gallery, New Delhi

2004 *Subtlety-Minimally*, curated by Marta Jakimowicz, Sakshi Gallery, New Delhi

2003 *Recent Works*, Gallery Threshold, New Delhi
Highlights, Sakshi Gallery, Mumbai

2001 *On the Edge of the Volume*, curated by Marta Jakimowicz, Sakshi Gallery and Alliance Française, Bangalore

2000 *Exile and Longing, Emerging Art Practices from Kerala*, Lakeeren Gallery, Mumbai
Bhoomi Geetha: A Song of the Earth, curated by Vidya Murthy, Red Chair Gallery, University of Missouri, Kansas City, Missouri

Acknowledgements

This monograph illuminates the many highlights of Prabhavathi Meppayil's artistic career. I am very grateful to the writers who have lent their beautiful words to this book: Mami Kataoka and Michaëla de Lacaze Mohrmann for their enlivening essay contributions, Wells Fray-Smith for her incisive interview, and Rosalind Krauss for graciously allowing us to reproduce her seminal essay in the context of this work. Additional thanks to Darryl Jingwen Wee for so eloquently translating Mami Kataoka's words.

I am also grateful to the team at A Practice for Everyday Life whose elegant design perfectly captures the intricacies of Meppayil's practice.

I would like to extend my warmest thanks to Margherita Ciocci, who has been instrumental in the making of this book, without whom it would not have been possible.

My sincere thanks to the global network of curators, writers, galleries and thinkers who have contributed so greatly to bringing attention to this important work: Deepak Ananth, Peter Benson Miller, Diana Campbell Betancourt, Benjamin H. D. Buchloh, Lexi Eberspacher, Massimiliano Gioni, Shanay Jhaveri, Aruna Keshav, Sunitha Kumar Emmart, Akiko Miki, Manuel Miseur, Rajeeb and Nadia Samdani, Esther Schipper, and Cornelia Tischmacher.

Lastly, thank you to my wonderful colleagues for their hard work and support: Gillian Canavan, Madeline Gilmore, Marly Hammer, Clare Preston, Amelia Redgrift, James Sadek, and Vincent Wilke.

Tamara Corm
Senior Director, Pace Gallery

Prabhavathi Meppayil would like to thank her family: Gopu, Bhagya, Geetha, Latha, Sudha, Sowmya, Abhishek, Akshay, Sneha and Sahana. She would also like to thank her studio family: Kiran, Jishith and Babu, whose immense efforts have helped in executing her work. Lastly, she is grateful to her Achchan and Amme, Gopalan and Radha, for being an embodiment of love, care and respect for others in the way they have lived.

Published on the occasion of
Prabhavathi Meppayil
May 12 – June 18, 2022

Pace Gallery
540 West 25th Street
New York

Artist's Quotations

16–17 from "Prabhavathi Meppayil with Laila Pedro," *The Brooklyn Rail*, December 2016.
60–61 from Wells Fray-Smith, "Being with the work and in the work: An Interview with Prabhavathi Meppayil," *Prabhavathi Meppayil* (New York: Pace Gallery, 2022), 93.
96–97 from Benjamin H. D. Buchloh, "Prabhavathi Meppayil: Redeeming Abstraction (under Duress)," *Prabhavathi Meppayil: nine seventeen* (New York: Pace Gallery, 2014), 41.
112–113 from Deepak Ananth, "White and Gold (and Copper and Light)," *Prabhavathi Meppayil: nine seventeen* (New York: Pace Gallery, 2014), 87.

Photography
© Belvedere, Vienna: p. 15. Jenni Carter: pp. 103–105. Davide Franceschini, courtesy The American Academy in Rome: pp. 94–95, 113–115, 117–119, 123. Courtesy Galleryske: pp. 74–75, 124–125. Francesco Galli: pp. 127–128, 131–133, 135. Damian Griffiths: pp. 6, 17–19, 21–22, 25–27, 29–43, 45–47, 49–53, 55–56, 58–60, 65–67, 69–70, 88. Damian Griffiths, courtesy of Drawing Room, 2017: pp. 86–87. Kerry Ryan McFate: pp. 97–101. © The Metropolitan Museum of Art. Image source: Art Resource, NY: p. 13. Courtesy Kiran Nadar Museum of Art: p. 73. © Andrea Rossetti: pp. 76–77, 79, 106–111. Randhir Singh, courtesy Dhaka Art Summit: pp. 61–63. Manoj Sudhakara: p. 91. © Yuichiro Tanaka: pp. 80–81, 83–84

Editor: Michaëla de Lacaze Mohrmann
Editorial Director: Gillian Canavan
Editorial Associate: Madeline Gilmore

Design and Art Direction: A Practice for Everyday Life
Copyediting: Elizabeth Franzen
Typeset in ABC Favorit Light
Printing: VeronaLibri

ISBN: 978-1-948701-41-9
Library of Congress Control Number: 2021925632

Available through ARTBOOK | D.A.P.
75 Broad Street, Suite 630 New York, NY 10004
www.artbook.com